333

ORACLE OF HEART WISDOM

Readings with Alana Fairchild

BLUE ANGEL®

BEAUTY EVERYWHERE

www.beautyeverywhere.com

333 ORACLE OF HEART WISDOM

Published by Blue Angel Publishing®
80 Glen Tower Drive, Glen Waverley
Victoria, Australia 3150
Email: info@blueangelonline.com
Website: www.blueangelonline.com

Edited by Marie Delbalso

ISBN: 978-1-925538-71-7

333 pathways of love, encouragement and strength are ready to flow from the Universe to the soul temple of your heart. These readings are here to help you remember your true self, to support you in becoming the light-bearing sacred rebel and empowered visionary that you were born to be. 333 holds the master frequency of playful power, creative consciousness and sacred connection. This frequency invites you to reach inwards and outwards, to lean into your truth and to reach out for the highest guidance the Universe can offer. Heart wisdom is founded on greater love to bring comfort, kindness and assurance alongside strong direction and deeper insight for growth, healing, joy and a brighter future for all.

– Alana

i

How to use the *333 Oracle of Heart Wisdom*

To consult the oracle, place your hand over your heart and formulate the question you wish to ask. If you don't have a specific question, you can simply ask, "What is the guidance I most need right now?"

Your question will always be answered, but not always in the way you expect! The 333 frequency will often suggest that you consider things from a higher perspective that can truly help you heal and find relief.

ii

Keep your heart and mind open to the answers you receive and allow the healing wisdom and unconditional love expressed in your reading to soak into your soul. You will always be given what you most need, so that you find the peace, courage and enthusiasm to live from your heart.

You may choose to do one of the guided readings from the three options below. To consult the oracle for others, simply have them say the suggested words, repeating after you if that's easier, and then choose the message for themselves. Add in your intuitive insight as you reflect on the meaning together.

iii

Reading for Yourself and Others

Immediate Insight Reading (one message)

The person giving and receiving the reading says aloud:

> *Connecting deeply with the heart, I/we open to the highest wisdom available, so I/we may find the true and best path forward.*

iv

The person receiving the reading then asks:

What do I most need to know at this time?

The person the reading is for then opens the book randomly and reads the relevant message. If the book opens at a page without a message, simply choose the closest message to that page. After reflecting on the message, close the reading with a simple thought of gratitude.

Heart Wisdom Reading (two messages)

The person giving and receiving the reading says:

> *Connecting deeply with the soul temple of the heart, I/we open to the highest perspective of truth and loving wisdom, for genuine healing and relief.*

The person receiving the reading then asks:

> *What does my heart want me to understand at this time?*

vi

The person the reading is for then opens the book randomly and reads the relevant message. If the book opens to a page without a message, simply choose the closest message. After reflecting on that message, it is time to choose a second message.

The person receiving the reading says:

> *What guidance will take my healing and manifestation to the next level?*

The person receiving the reading again opens the book at random and reads the relevant message. After reflecting on that message, it is time to close the session.

vii

The person giving the reading can close with this prayer:

> *May heart wisdom continue to unfold and attract ample blessings into your life for the true benefit of all beings. Namaste.*

viii

The 333 In-depth Reading (three messages)

The person giving and the person receiving the reading says:

I/we connect with the depth of the heart, where soul wisdom originates and generates answers to any and all problems. I/we now open myself/ourselves to receive authentic, unconditionally loving and helpful, healing guidance at this time, for the greatest good of all beings.

The person receiving the reading asks:

What heart wisdom can help me most, now?

ix

The person receiving the reading opens the book at random and reads the relevant message. If the book opens at a page without a message, go to the message on the nearest page. After reflecting on the message, it is time to choose the second message.

The person receiving the reading asks:

> *How can I maximise my positive potential, in this moment?*

The person receiving the reading opens the book at random and reads the relevant message. After reflecting on that message, it is time to choose the final message for the session.

א

The person receiving the reading asks:

How can I live my best possible future?

The person receiving the reading again opens the book at random and reads the relevant message. After reflecting on that message, it is time to close the session.

The person giving the reading can say the following and invite the person receiving the reading to repeat the relevant portion:

To integrate this reading and attract continued assistance from unconditionally loving and wise sources, I/we say, "May countless blessings unfold in my heart for the highest benefit to all beings.'

The person giving the reading can close the session by putting their hands at their heart in a simple prayer position and saying:

Namaste.

The Messages

1 You Are Being Helped

When you feel strongly about helping others and living with as much freedom, courage and love as you can, you have spiritually dedicated yourself as a vehicle through which the Universe will weave magic and healing in the world. Your decision to give and create something constructive attracts an abundance of spiritual resources to you. Lean into that. Trust that there is more than enough assistance available for all, including you and any matter you might be concerned about.

2 Hidden Blessings Will Be Revealed

There will be times when we feel as though nothing is flowing. You might encounter obstacles and closed doors. This is not a sign that you should worry, but a time to look beyond what appears to be. Trust in the power of the Universe to work things out in the best possible way, according to a timing that will work best for all, including you. You don't have to know what that solution will look like or when it will happen. You do need to allow yourself to be guided from within, trusting that the Universe is always working for your greatest good. For now, have patience and hope.

3 Let Your Life Happen

Your path has to twist and turn a little sometimes. There are invisible obstacles to be avoided through grace, elements that need to be integrated and things that need to happen, so the bigger picture can come together. As you tune into your heart and feel for your connection to the Universe, you will find it easier to relax into the unfoldment of your destiny. It is a natural synchronicity of people, opportunities and events, according to a higher plan. It is all working out. Stay true to your path and have faith.

4

Commit to Your Dream

Take care not compromise your dreams out of doubt, fear or guilt. Hold true to the light that inspires you within your heart. Remind yourself that the pain of the past is not an indication of what your future holds. Even the most difficult situations can and will heal. Give yourself permission to explore the simple things that bring you happiness and pleasure. Create light in your life and it will support you as you take your authentic life journey. It will sometimes ask you to have the courage to go through challenges that will awaken your true self and manifest your light in this world.

5 Embrace Unfamiliar Territory

As you grow toward the fulfilment of your divine destiny, you may need guidance to help you through unfamiliar situations. This is a sign that you are broadening your spiritual horizons. You and many others will benefit as you move beyond your comfort zone. Let the call to new adventure stir your heart. Seek wise companions and choose to gently, but firmly, cast aside voices of fear. Give yourself and others a precious gift of freedom through the unconditional forgiveness of whatever has been. It is not what you have done but what you choose to do now that matters. You have great power in this moment.

6 You Are Blessed

You might judge yourself or your situation, but actually you are making great progress. If you feel like you are stumbling from time to time, it is because you are growing, you are breaking free from past constraints and becoming more fully and freely yourself. This is brave. Be proud, even of your stumbles. You do not need to criticise yourself or the process in any way. Remember that whatever your heart yearns for is what the Universe wants for you, too. The way it can best manifest might be different to what you expect, and that's okay. You can trust in your unfolding destiny. It is safe and wise to allow it to move you.

7 It Shall Manifest

Our true progress on our path can be hidden under the ordinary day-to-day and not-quite-feeling-you-are-there-yet moments. Those are the all-important times when we are building our spiritual muscles. Faith, courage, trust, determination, commitment, patience and serenity grow in the face of challenge and uncertainty. As these spiritual muscles grow and exert themselves, the physical world responds by taking shape and responding to our inner power. Your soul is coming to life in the world, and your heart's desires will manifest. You may fear sometimes, but there is a greater hand guiding your course and it is safe to trust it. Keep going.

8

No Need to Worry

Fear tends to add to one's confusion and makes things seem far more complicated than they are in truth. The Universe knows what you need, and you are being guided toward fulfilment, daily. Everything you have and are right now, is enough to take your next step. So, do what you can do now. Trust in the power of your process. Whether you recognise it or not, you are making progress. Even when your mind doubts or worries about choices made or an uncertain future, you can choose to trust that it is all working out, somehow. What you need shall be provided. Keep connecting to your true self. Know that you are guided and protected so that you can take your life journey.

9 Answered Prayer

The oracle brings soothing guidance that something more beautiful wants to manifest in your world. Reassure yourself that any chaos or disorder is the Universe speaking to you, saying, "I want to improve something for you, let me do it." Here's a secret: If you don't try to control it, you may actually come to enjoy the creative, sometimes messy, process of healing change. The changes happening for you are part of how your prayers are being answered. Do not fight against the creation of your own dream! In time, you will see that what seemed like a problem was actually part of the solution.

10

Let Go

When we hold on too tight, we can suffocate what we want to see flourish in our life. It can be so helpful to loosen our grip psychologically and emotionally, and to allow for endings to happen. Those endings are the beginnings of new chapters and are guiding you closer to what you seek. Stay connected to your hope. Blessings of healing and comfort are seeking their way in to your heart. No matter how difficult or final things may seem, these blessings will ensure that love and light shall prevail. Let hope nurture your innermost being with comfort and peace. There is another way, but it is yet to be consciously perceived. All is well.

11 Rely Upon Inner Values Rather Than Social Opinions

The opinions of a collective, be it a culture or other social tribe, can be so widely-accepted that they are falsely recognised as being a kind of law. With the weight of so many in agreement, beliefs and judgements may appear to be worthy of respect. However, the number of people holding an opinion does not proportionally increase its degree of truth, wisdom or helpfulness. Often it is quite the opposite. Living an authentic life, as you were born to live it, will often require you to have the courage to break with societal conditioning and live according to your own inner values. Don't worry what other people are going to think or say. Trust your heart and seek your own counsel.

12

Empower Your Hopefulness

We can make great progress on our spiritual path on an entirely inner level, with no evidence that the outer world shall ever give way to the luminosity and spiritual power growing steadily within. Maybe all we see in our outer world are blocks and obstacles! These are the times to be spiritually stubborn by applying ourselves to our inner work, summoning hope and divine defiance, and recognising that it is not a matter of luck but a law of nature that our efforts will eventually bring transformation. Stay hopeful and expect your beautiful breakthrough to happen at the best time and in the best way.

13 Successful Transition

Life is often experienced as a transitional process, where we are no longer bound by the past but are yet to feel fully grounded in a new cycle. Remembering that we do not need to force a premature rebirth, that all things happen in harmony with a wise and loving divine timing, allows us to continue to work toward manifesting our desires, whilst settling with peace and curiosity in the present. Balancing acceptance for what is, with trust that it is serving your soul in some delicious and generous way, can allow you to cultivate hope and positive anticipation for your future. This is not your final destination, but you can still enjoy being here.

14 Be Guided by Your Wildness

Wildness has an instinct to it - an instinct for when to rest, trust, be cautious, be patient and allow things to take shape, and for when to take the initiative and act with bold confidence. This instinctive inner wildness is not bound by what you, or other people, may think or wish. It responds to what is and therein lies its genius. There is a truth to be acknowledged. That is not a cause for anxiety. There is a way to grow in wisdom through acknowledging this truth, and perhaps a simple step to take in response, also. You are more equipped to deal with the circumstances in your life than you realise. Give yourself a chance to demonstrate your competence. Also, remember that you don't need to anticipate how things are going to work out in the long term. Deal with what is now and keep your heart optimistically open to what shall eventually be.

15 Invite the Universe to Your Party

There is a childlike innocence and wonder that dwells within you, no matter what your age may be. That open, curious part of your being teaches you that you haven't got it all figured out, and that is a good thing. Whilst planning can be helpful, one does well to leave enough space for the Universe to step in and realign our direction and focus in order to accomplish a superior outcome. Be like the child, open and curious, even excited, to be dazzled by the Universe evoking something wonderful in your life. Through your optimistic attitude you invite the Universe to demonstrate its extraordinary ability to weave everything together perfectly, surprisingly and generously.

16 Do the Opposite of What Your Ego Suggests

When we are challenged, hurt or uncertain, the ego will generally guide us to lash out in anger or to defend ourselves from the perceived onslaught out of fear. This approach creates unnecessary and unhelpful barriers against the inflow of spiritual intervention, healing and grace. When you want to close yourself down or turn away from life, take a moment to consider opening and allowing your heart to expand so that it is larger than the challenge at hand. Ask the Universe for help. Allow peace, reassurance and some divine ingenuity and resourcefulness to save the day, and it will. If you've stumbled off track, you'll come back strong and continue with more confidence than ever before.

17 Work Smarter Rather Than Harder

There is a time and place for hard work. At the right time, in response to genuine inner urgings of the soul, much can be accomplished through commitment and discipline. Yet there are also times when pushing harder simply wears one out and accomplishes little. Give up force, which is based on doubt, and embrace the wisdom that is founded on unwavering confidence in your destiny. You are not being asked to become passive, but to be fully responsible for intelligently drawing on your resources and allowing time for replenishment and inspiration. Great abundance is created when a willing human asks a loving Universe to deliver all that is needed for success to occur for the greatest good of all. You don't have to do everything on your own. Let yourself be supported. Let the way become a little easier.

18 Take Care of Yourself

Have you been too hard on yourself about some matter or other? It is time to take sanctuary in the love and comfort of the heart, rather than beating one's self with the worries of the mind. The heart knows exactly how to accomplish whatever needs to happen. It possesses the will and the power to rectify what is not correct, to allow you to take your journey as you so choose and to soften the roughness of your demands on yourself. Then the Universe will be empowered to generously mirror such kindness back to you. Take your mind off things. Let spiritual grace teach you how to experience the generosity and comfort of love so you can feel genuinely cared for by yourself and the Universe.

19

Relieving Joy Deficiency

There are times when even the most noble and meaningful pursuits can become wearying to the passionate heart. What once inspired and vitalised you may become burdensome and draining. That does not mean that such goals and pursuits suddenly lack value or are no longer right for you. More often, it means that in your enthusiasm to make progress, you have been pushing too hard and have become disconnected from your inner joy. Can you reconnect with your playfulness? Engage in something silly, good-natured and fun. Make a time when you can set aside serious matters, so that you may return to your pursuits with a refreshed viewpoint and mountains have mysteriously transformed into molehills. Give yourself a chance and you shall naturally assume a more constructive and positive outlook.

20 Perfect Timing

In the realm of divine timing, there is no such thing as a late bloomer. There is only the perfectly timed and natural ripening of the soul that happens over the course of one's life. One does not need to be concerned about age so much as taking one's journey with courage and confidence, remembering that all things happen at the best time. It is never too late to begin, to finish, to love, to realise something, to forgive, to smile or to free yourself and others from fear and doubt. So, why not surrender any concerns with grace now? You can be secure in the reassurance that your time to bloom has already been reserved and prepared by the Universe. Your time shall come.

21

No Need to Doubt

If you cannot allow yourself to trust that a greater loving power is stimulating and guiding your path, then you will find the process of living, with all its uncertainties and mysteries, to be more painful than it need be. You might sometimes feel like you are going crazy with doubt - doubting yourself, doubting what life is bringing to you and insecure about your future. Shield yourself from the opinions of others and your own uncertain mind. Seek peaceful sanctuary in the spiritual presence that is always available to you, deep within your heart. There you will find reassurance and encouragement. This oracle brings you the message that no matter what your fears or doubts may be conjuring, everything is working out according to a higher loving plan. Trust that everything is going to be okay (or absolutely wonderful!).

22 Warrior, Lay Down Thy Weapons

Not one other human may know the full extent of the wars that have been raging within your soul, yet the Universe sees and knows all and loves you without condition. Tension and conflict are part of our lives, but not our entire lives. You can choose not to allow unnecessarily destructive energies to overcome your spirit. There is a very real and loving spiritual grace that wants to enter and comfort your heart and bring peace to your mind. Use your warrior strength to step away from conflict. Choose a radical letting go that will enable you to feel completely immersed in spiritual grace, so that nothing else can touch you. Let the field of peace that such grace generates fill you up and create spaciousness around you. A new way is emerging for you now. Acknowledge the past and what you have learned but don't reserve a place for it in the present moment or believe that it belongs to your future. It is time to end the war and allow yourself to thrive.

23 Fortitude for Freedom

You have the mental strength to let go of a conflict and break the shackles of shame and blame. You have the courage within you to respect that each being, including yourself, has the innate spiritual right to choose how to live this precious gift of life. How we live will always involve making mistakes - also known as learning opportunities. Remembering this sets an internal boundary and frees you to recognise that the actions of others are not a reflection of you, but of their own inner state of being, their choices and how they wish to live. You are free to choose what you invite into your world, and your heart. You are free to respectfully, but firmly, cast aside all that does not belong to you.

24 Hidden Progress

A sailor swiftly approaching an undiscovered shore, may have no evidence of progress being made until the very last moment! Similarly, we can be making great strides on our spiritual path, steadily lessening the distance from our goals, but not see any signs or confirmation until the very moment is upon us. There is a choice to be made. You can give up in the absence of external validation, or continue on, based on nothing more than your intuitive sense that it is correct to do so. You do not lack courage, but at times you lack certainty. Know that your intuitive inclinations are worthy of your trust. You are making greater progress than you currently recognise. Do not be deterred from that which you seek.

25

Veil of Mystery

There will be times when we lack clarity. In such moments, the intellect often rushes in to save the day, analysing what is known, in order to discover what is not yet knowable. That creates further confusion. There is a spiritual veil over part of your life at present. What is being hidden is not something to fear but something you will embrace in due course. So why is it being hidden from your knowledge at this time? Knowing the end of a story before reading it may soothe an anxious mind, but it also prevents one from growing through the journey. Allow yourself to be at peace in the face of the unknown. These circumstances are only temporary. Your story shall have its happy fulfilment, whether in the way you expect, at the time you expect, or not. Your answers will come, but for now the guidance is to be patient.

26

From Enthusiasm to Wisdom

Sometimes in our enthusiasm to accomplish a task, we attempt to set the wheels in motion prematurely. How does one know whether life is calling for bold initiative or patient receptiveness to a future insight that will prove not only to be helpful, but essential to one's success? Intuition. For a moment, put to one side what you wish reality looked like right now or what you think you should do, and tune into what you feel is the most authentic and in-tune-with-your-soul action (or non-action) for you at this time. Then trust in that. As you slow down and take the pressure off yourself, you will make a wise decision.

27 Find Your Centre

Even when your entire life seems to be spinning into the chaos of change, upheaval, healing and transformation (or just the first two), you need not fear. Within you is a remarkably powerful and sustaining spiritual centre. Seek out that quiet and still place within. It is strong enough to steady you, even during the wildest and most unpredictable twists of fate. Ground yourself spiritually and know that the disarray is breaking down an old order so that a new and more aligned way of being can manifest itself. Sometimes one's life meets the Universe's plans and an alchemical upheaval is the result. It is rarely predictable, but it is trustworthy. Whether you recognise it or not right now, good things are happening.

28 Resurgence

The mind is capable of compelling fabrications. You can talk yourself into believing a dire outcome is inevitable, only to have a sudden jolt of clarity a short time later, when you realise everything is actually working out perfectly. This oracle denotes the resurgence of a near-abandoned ideal. Perhaps a dream has been a long time coming and you have taken the prolonged delay as a sign to jump ship. Be reminded that all cherished dreams eventually find their moment to take shape in the world. Do not attempt to rally and force an outcome. Allow hope to keep your heart open to what shall be.

29

Realists Believe in Magic

Don't let your pessimistic opinions put a stranglehold on the generosity of the Universe! Why decide in advance that something cannot be, or that something must be according to your current (limited) viewpoint? You could allow your life to become a pliable instrument for the magical, the miraculous and the gracious. Why rush in to prove that life is hard and nothing good ever happens or that it's all going to hell in a handbasket (as the charmingly quirky expression goes). The cynics of this world entertain the notion that they have life figured out. That's not possible. It's not even much fun. Why not be a realist and prepare yourself for the delightful tricks the Universe has been hiding up its celestial sleeve?

30 Lost Child Found

The Universal Mother is a loving consciousness and spiritual sanctuary for all beings. We especially need her when we are afraid and anxious for ourselves or another, feel judged or betrayed, helpless or lost, uneasy or uncertain and find it difficult to trust - particularly when a difficult situation is upon us. When we consciously recognise the unbreakable spiritual bond between every being and the Universal Mother, we can use our care and concern to ask her for protection and grace for all beings, especially for those caught too deep in their suffering to ask for themselves. She reassures you now that whatever your concern for yourself or another being, she is holding, caring, nurturing and loving that being, and you. Do not fret. Trust in her loving and far-reaching power.

31 Call to Becoming

Divine discontent has a legitimate place, even within an otherwise grateful and happy heart. It is the inner urging toward one's own growth that leads us directly into the unfamiliar, and perhaps uncomfortable, experiences that are pathways to embodying more of one's being. Sometimes the mind continues to hold on to what is known, if only for the comfort of familiarity, long after the heart feels stifled and yearns for more aliveness. All that is divinely destined for you, needs a chance to manifest. Don't hold yourself back from life. Give yourself over to the inner creative genius of your unfoldment. It is your own brilliant spirit urging you on. So much more is meant for you.

32 The Power of the Past is Lessening

The past is truly over. You might struggle to feel free from what once was but be reassured that any power the past once held over you is swiftly receding, just as your strength of presence in the now is strengthening. With this oracle comes a blessing for beginning a new cycle in your life, starting now. You have the power to move on from the past as a new person, with an enhanced sense of wellbeing, vitality and authenticity. There is no need for shame or blame. There is just your precious and beautiful life to live. Honour your emotional journey - including the need to grieve and reflect - and embrace this blessing of release with peace in your heart. Know that the past has no power to hold you back.

33

Freewill

You have the freewill to live as you choose. However, the repercussions of our choices are not always helpful. These consequences are not always foreseeable. There is no need to be fearful as this message is not a warning. Rather it is an explanation. Spirit will intercede on your behalf to prevent movement along a path that may have seemed like a great idea at the time, but due to circumstances not yet known to you, would not have constructively furthered your progress. If you are feeling blocked or thwarted, shift your frustration to gratitude for being protected from something that wouldn't have been good for you at all. Trust that what is meant to come to you shall come, and it will genuinely be able to enhance your happiness and fulfilment, rather than promising much in potential but delivering little in reality. Set your intentions in motion but detach from outcomes, knowing that only what truly serves will find its way into your world.

34 The Way Forward Can Seem Backwards

As we grow in spiritual maturity, we become more present. Presence shows us what is really happening. As we develop presence, we may feel as though we are going through a healing crisis. We may face issues we believed we had already put behind us. This is not a sign to delve back into the past. It is an opportunity to hold compassionate space in the present moment. In this space, we might see things with more clarity and awareness and come to realise that we have more choices, more wisdom, and more strength than we previously recognised. When you remember that your healing is a sign of progress and development, you can allow it to unfold with serenity in your heart. You are closer to a breakthrough than you realise. Stay committed to your healing journey.

35

Nurture the Dream

To bring a cherished dream to life, one must be willing to let go of the perfect fantasy and allow the stainless vision to become a bit muddy and broken, like a seed cracking open in Mother Earth's richly generative soil. This is how things grow from idea to reality. The spiralling path to fulfilment will likely surprise you again and again. Yet, the nourishing true essence of your dreams can be detected in the most unexpected outer expressions. You do not need to direct or control the way your dreams manifest. Rather, allow yourself to be guided, inspired and empowered. Opportunities shall arise and pathways shall open. The desires in your heart were lovingly placed there by divine design so they might come to life through you. Trust this. Your dreams are meant to be.

36

Infinite Resourcefulness

There is no limit to what grace renders possible. This is the realm of the miraculous, where a lost thought is reborn, and the pathway once denied suddenly opens without effort or strain. It is the right connection at the right time, and all things falling into place, effortlessly. Such is the tangible outcome of the invisible handiwork of the masterful, divine feminine creatrix at play. You do not need to orchestrate your success. Get out of the way. Attend to your work and trust in the manifesting power of the sacred.

37 Unconditional Trust

Trust is unconditional. Trust is faith. We need it when something isn't going according to our plan and we feel afraid or anxious. We need it when we are willing to grow spiritually, to reach out and to lean into an intelligence, a sacredness, a presence that is greater than our limited human perspectives and plans. Trust is the spiritual trip switch that opens us to divine intervention and genius. Trust doesn't require passivity. It asks that we fully participate in life, letting our heart acknowledge that our opinions on how things should be often need to give way to reasons that we do not understand. Even so, we can instinctively know that we are loved by a powerful and protective higher intelligence and that our life path is unfolding according to a deep, soul-nurturing grace.

38

Boldly Go Forth

There is wisdom in allowing life to unfold according to its own timing, conserving energy and moving in harmony with the greater power of life itself. However, one needs to take care not to misapply such wisdom and become afraid to take the actions that are the building blocks for one's dreams. Acceptance is not inactivity, but it does require us to cultivate detachment from outcome. This frees us to care, to be passionate and bold, and to not hold back due to fear of failure, nor to push from a place of neediness. Allow your inspired, intuitive heart to fearlessly claim your right to rest and when you sense it is the right time, to act boldly with confidence.

39

Wise Use of Will

There is only so much that effort alone can accomplish. Giving your imagination the freedom to run wild or engage in silliness can replenish your physical, emotional and mental resources. Relaxation and the freedom to simply be in the moment, moved by inner spontaneity rather than willpower, takes the pressure off. If the flow is not there and the spark will not ignite no matter how much effort is applied, then the wise use of will is likely be to step back and switch off for a time. Even delays can be part of a forward moving process. Just like the surfer waiting for the next wave, you'll sense the moment when the energy begins to stir, so you can switch back on and rise with the movements of life. Trust in your timing.

40 Across the Waters Another World Beckons

To cross the waters requires that we leave the safety of what we have known, enduring a period of potentially unsettling transition. If we can bear the process for long enough, we will touch the new shore. Then we need the willingness to begin again, in a new world, with openness to yet further uncertainty and possibility. The oracle advises you to be open to the new, to continue to seek, and to be at peace with the discomfort and not-knowingness that tend to accompany such a state. What it will bring to you, is worth it. There is an expansion into as yet unknown realms that is meant for you. Answer the call of beckoning worlds with a heartfelt yes. Take the journey.

41

See the Signs

The Universe is always communicating with us. When we drop preconceived ideas about when or how we should receive our sign, and we relax and open to receiving, the messages flow readily. The logical mind attempts to grasp the infinite and concretise it or tries to tell it what to do and when. That obstructs the free flow of communication between your heart and the Universe. Authentic signs trigger a sense of inner knowing. They do not need to be justifiable or explainable. You'll feel spontaneously, palpably, and often unexpectedly connected to something greater and reassured by the connection. Trust when the heart is moved by an encounter with the numinous. And if you've been asking for a sign, consider this to be it.

42

Brave Individual

Collective beliefs can tend toward ostracising or even victimising the 'other'. Sometimes a collective may even attempt to cast you as that 'other'. Within your own heart and mind, don't buy into such nonsense. You are your own sovereign being. You do not need to define yourself, nor accept the projected definitions of others, based on belonging to, or not belonging to, any group. All humans belong to the human collective, the Earth Mother and spirit. Honour your right to respect yourself and affirm your own sense of greater belonging. Do not accept abuse from another out of a misplaced sense of compassion. That is not kind or helpful to anyone. You do not need fear or hate to protect yourself. Be you. Choose how you wish to live, feel and be. Trust that you are lovable and that you are meant to be you.

43 Connect and Co-Create

You have a path to walk this lifetime that is solely yours. Yet you are also part of a collective. How might you acknowledge your belonging and your individuality? What would sharing your essence and receiving from others, without losing connection with yourself, feel or look like? Without abandoning the need for solitude and inner reflection, value what it is that you have to offer and receive in connection and in the process of collective co-creation. Your individual soul scent can intertwine with others to create a most exquisite perfume for all to enjoy. Take ample time out for yourself, but do not hide yourself away.

44 Seek Thy Tribe and Treasure Thy Freedom

Your soul tribes are the karmic groups through which you shall learn and grow. Meeting with your soul tribes may feel like a homecoming or in some way deeply life-changing, whether it is a long-term or short-term involvement for you this lifetime. This oracle encourages you to explore soul connections, discerning when a deep and enduring soul commitment can truly be made, and when your authentic journey entails you being more like respectful visitors, passing through each other's lives. In your quest to connect, be clear about how much you value your authenticity over the need to conform in order to belong. Reach out but remember to stay true to your path and treasure the gift of your freedom.

45

Brilliance of Your Body

Something precious on the spiritual level wants to come to life, taking form in the physical world. An inspiration, plan or idea is ready to become a reality. Your body is the sacred instrument through which this manifestation can occur. Allow your body to be immersed in this inspiration, to hold, amplify and radiate its frequency. What does it feel like? How could you live in a way that honours that feeling? The more presence, love and care you give to your body, the stronger this broadcast shall become and the more dramatically the power of attraction will open up for your successful organic translation of dream into reality. Trust your body and in what is meant to be.

46

Scar Wisdom

There are some wisdoms that are only gained from our most challenging life experiences. Many lessons in life can be mastered through gentler approaches, but upon rare occasions, an initiation, taking us into the depths of our fears or doubts, is what holds the capacity to help us break free and become truly connected to something greater, becoming empowered in relationship with our own courageous, self-renewing spirit. The oracle advises that you have the inner capacity to recover from any trauma, no matter how deeply it affected you. Your scars will heal, and you will distil wisdom of great value from your experience. You have the strength to move through this time and are heading toward a gentler future.

47 Ending of a War

Sometimes an issue can continue for so long that the thought of it no longer featuring in our life never crosses our mind. We assume its continued existence and that we have to learn to deal with it as an unwanted but unavoidable constant. At best, we might fantasise about the situation becoming a bit easier to manage if we can grow enough. This oracle speaks of a more dramatic shift, a complete release from a legacy of negativity that once held you captive. Even if the habit of struggle has become ingrained and such a too-wearying battle has begun to poison your heart with defeat or bitterness, the Universe is stepping in to protect you. No matter how unlikely it may seem, you shall be freed from this cycle of struggle.

48

Night Blooming Soul

From the desert's night-blooming flower, we learn that each creation has its own unique timing so that it may thrive. There are times when on the surface of things, conditions seem to be hostile toward the soul. Respect and honouring of light, goodness, dignity and grace may seem to become a rarity. However, the genius of growth is not bound by logic nor by appearances. Nor can it be controlled by fear or violence. Growth happens improbably, regularly, spontaneously and miraculously. Do not be hoodwinked into negativity or doubt. Your time to bloom shall happen. You shall thrive.

49

Give Your Spirit Feet

Allowing the abundant mental and spiritual energies swirling around your head to settle and ground increases your vitality, giving you the ability to anchor your spirit into the world where it can manifest its light and do the most good. The stronger and deeper you ground spirit into your body, the more you become as the Tree of Life, growing deep and strong roots, so that it can stand strong in the face of any storm and provide shelter to support life's creatures. You are capable of more than dreaming. You are capable of embodiment. Keep your head plugged into the inspirational energies of the sky, whilst grounding your feet upon this sacred earth. Be here and walk your path. There is much of value that you are capable of accomplishing.

50

Broken Trust Repaired

After a betrayal or disappointment, it is a conscious choice to trust again. Even helpful twists of fate can temporarily trigger issues around safety and security. If a sense of foreboding is arising, you are being given an opportunity to switch from fear-based to trust-based reality. Whether the darkness that you have been encountering is arising from within your own mind or from those around you, you are reassured by this oracle that you have, within your own heart, a special power to overcome it. That power is trust - in the Universe and in yourself. You've been through more difficult times than this and triumphed. Hold the intention and be open to receive whatever assistance you need to attract such support. Also be at peace in the acknowledgement of your own power, grace and inner strength.

51 Ascension Blessing

The Universe is giving you a blessing that will enable a project, idea or cycle to begin readily and easily. It can be a peculiar quirk of human nature to dismiss the easy successes as less worthy. This oracle guides you to use your wisdom instead of allowing such foolishness to overtake the process. Let the Universe make things easier for you. Wholeheartedly embrace the free pass being offered to you. Whether you realise it or not, you have generated this merit. Know that as you heal and grow spiritually, other beings gain benefit, too. If you have been struggling, expect a fortunate adjustment in your affairs. If you are contemplating a new path or project, consider this an affirmation and commit to your path. You are being led toward a new way, with more grace and less fear. Move freely toward it with a trusting and peaceful heart.

52

Consciousness of Conditioning

When we feel stuck in a situation not of our choosing - especially when the situation feels negative - we often need to bring some previously unconscious conditioning into conscious awareness. At a deep level, we may have been denied the right to be respected. Becoming aware of this allows for the possibility of a new, less defensive and less aggressive way of being. Just because you've believed something to be true in the past, doesn't mean that it's beyond question now. Can you shed a layer of your conditioned mind, so that more gentleness toward self, and perhaps even others, can soften your world view? You can overcome a persistent negative pattern now. Doing so begins with the realisation that such spiritual success is possible.

53

The Tao

When you grow, you do not only do so in one direction, or in one part of your life. When you are in a positive process of expansion, there will be a testing time. Sometimes you will feel sure of your progress, at other times it will seem like the opposite! When one is facing challenges that feel familiar, it is worth asking, "Can I respond differently to how I once would have reacted?" There is no need to be disheartened when you feel like you are encountering something that you thought you had put behind you. Nor should new challenges dissuade you from continuing your journey. Instead, be reassured that you are growing in all directions, clearing your path, and becoming ready for the wonder of what is next. Trust in life's inherent goodness and grace.

54

Soul Talent

Nurturing a raw talent through exploration and expression transforms it into a potentially sacred offering to the world. Even abundant, natural talent may evoke testing from the Universe so that the depths of beauty and ability can be distilled. Part of your journey this lifetime involves the discovery and development of a particular soul ability. It is a precious pearl, at times hard won. However, it can bring about incredible joy and fulfilment for you and for others. Commit yourself to the development of your soul abilities with courage, detachment and a sense of humour. There is a higher purpose to your inner development. Whether it seems practical or not, there is great value in your journey and good things shall come of it.

55

Process to Progress

There has been a lot going on in your mind, maybe a lot going on around you, too. There is great benefit to be gained from taking time to process, reflect and release - before taking in any further information. There is something nourishing and life-affirming, clarifying and helpful that is waiting to be tapped into. To do so, step back from the day-to-day world and don't push forward, but rather take a moment to create the space to journey within. Hidden gifts shall become apparent and with the patience to rest and percolate, swifter progress shall ultimately unfold, along a wise course and in harmony with greater cycles of divine timing. Take some time to process and you'll make faster, happier progress.

56 Graceful Release, Ecstatic Embrace

Your karmic tribe consists of those souls with whom you are travelling spiritually this lifetime, to accomplish healing. These are the beings with whom we feel profound connection, often without knowing exactly why or what the nature of the connection might be. One can hold space for such connections with presence, acknowledging their depth, and trusting that a way work to through whatever may need to be resolved will always be shown, whether that be on an emotional or spiritual level. Sometimes an advanced soul will incarnate into a particular group to help heal it from within, through taking their own spiritual journey. Trust in the connections that arise and fall away. There is a sacred purpose behind all that is unfolding.

57

Drink Deeply Thirsty Soul

Some souls are satisfied with flighty fancies and passing highs. Some, such as your own, have a bolder appetite for life. The extraordinary may be perceived in the apparently ordinary and the rapture of aliveness may be experienced side by side with quiet, non-demanding, unaffected presence. Life loves such lovers, providing them with what is needed to satisfy their spiritual hunger. Let your ego give way with its plans and expectations, to what life is providing now. It may not seem to be in line with what you imagined should or could be, but life has a far grander plan intended for you, one that will truly satisfy the deepest yearnings of your soul.

58 Wrong Things Made Right

When the ego has a stranglehold on the soul, spiritual intervention will manifest to counter it, dislodging the grip of false view and unconscious momentum, providing a way back to the heart. The ego lacks imagination whilst the soul is capable of dreaming the most extraordinarily beautiful dreams. This process of ego sacrifice for soul success can perhaps be described as losing the battle to win the war. Give up your temporary frustration and find peace in your heart, letting go, and allowing for needs to be. What was not right is being corrected. Stay open to changing perspectives and unexpected realignments. What is meant to be, shall be.

59 Deep Blue Cloak of The Sacred Feminine

She wraps you beneath her deep blue cloak of protection, shielding you from what you think you want and need, but would - if permitted - actually lead you into harm and further suffering. In time you will be so grateful for what is happening right now. Despite the pain, if the attachment is deep, a blessing beyond your wildest imaginings is presently unfolding. The testing time is rapidly drawing to a close and light, grace and relief shall pour forth swiftly into your heart. Open your mind to the generous goodwill that divine beings are holding in their hearts for you. There is much to be grateful for and so much grace that supports you. You are safe from harm.

60

Badass Lightworkers

When one has enough passion to devote to easing the suffering on this planet, one can become tired at heart. The fatigued heart can become susceptible to the fear-based perceptions of the mind - judgement of others or oneself, fear that humanity will never heal or evolve, or doubt that you'll ever find or fulfil the higher purpose that you sense is part of your destiny. There are countless mantras, prayers and blessings on behalf of all beings being offered at all times. Such goodwill can be felt as vibrations in your bones, helping to shift the course of your path and open your heart to astonishing grace. You can add your own good thoughts and prayers to that sacred choir. Trust in the badass power of the light.

61 From the West to the East

Just as the Sun sets in the west, and rises again in the east, so too has your own inner spiritual sun - your soul - broken the bonds of a cycle, ready to begin anew. There is a wisdom within your heart that understands one needs courage to invite in the new. It involves going through a dark night, for how else can the dawn break? Give over any regret or concern about the past. Honour your pain but take care that you do not allow yourself to dwell on the negative. Giving undue time or energy from the present moment to that which belongs in the past can undermine your strength. Set a boundary with what has been and enter fully into this moment. Something beautiful is happening for you. Fixation on the past may prevent you from recognising the movement and call of grace in your life. Summon your compassion and also your courage. You can turn to face the light with optimism in your heart.

62

Match Made in Heaven

The Universe is a skilful and compassionate matchmaker, drawing together an endless array of sacred relationships and connections to encourage growth, and allow for the experience of love in new ways. If one retains an open heart to such workings, the Universe will offer opportunities for healing as well as exciting, enlightening experiences. This oracle indicates spiritual significance in matters of relationship. This can relate to healing in your relationship with yourself and with life, perhaps learning to feel safe and loved from within. It can extend to spiritually inspired breakthroughs of awareness in current relationships, so that soul healing may take place for all involved. This oracle also indicates that future connections shall unfold at the right time and be instrumental in the unfolding of divine destinies for many beings.

63

Sacred Revelation

Allow yourself to be shown the intricate spiritual purpose of a relationship, or another matter of concern, seeing it as it is revealed, rather than attempting to shape it according to your will. You will then be able to benefit from the divine gift being offered as you start to understand and accept it, rather than try to control or avoid it. Sometimes painful issues will arise, but it is in order to heal and gain access to a new way of being. The inner eye can see with perfect clarity because it trusts in what shall be shown. Revelation happens when we allow space for it. There is no need to try and force an outcome or an understanding. You shall have your answers at the right time, and you shall be able to work with that knowledge in a loving and wise way. You shall see the truth that will bring relief to your heart and clarity to your mind.

64

Wisdom of the Non-Rational

The non-rational is the intuitive, instinctive knowing of the heart, unconstrained by logic. This does not mean that it is irrational, unfounded or unsound. The non-rational is a wisdom that flows from a deeper holistic perception. Perhaps you are already sensing something is happening at a subtle level. Even without a shred of physical evidence to support it, non-rational knowing resonates as truth. It cuts through intellectual assessment and reveals what is. You can allow your sensitivities to grant you access to deeper truths that can help you find your way, in alignment with a greater guiding wisdom. There is no greater happiness or deeply satisfying success than that which arises when you are proceeding in harmony with the Universe.

65 Commit to Closure

The promise of the new can be enticing. The intoxicating blend of hope, inspiration and optimism can seem irresistible. There are many beautiful ideas and dreams to conjure up, yet limited time to bring them all to life. A vivid imagination, open to possibilities, can keep us youthful and vital. However, that same questing nature can distract us from fulfilling our purpose if fear, boredom or lack of commitment is what is driving it. Sometimes the thrill of the new needs to be placed aside so that the joyful fulfilment of heartfelt ideas can come to life. There are many beautiful adventures on your spiritual horizon, but you can only approach them by taking the journey, step by step, in the here and now. Earn your next creative leap by attending to what needs to be done.

66

Happiness

To learn to feel joy in our hearts, without needing to have a particular reason for it (other than, say, the extraordinary experience of aliveness), is the beginning of access to authentic spiritual empowerment. Our Universe loves the unreasonable dreamers, optimists and healers, so much so that it will unconditionally support such crazy love-wisdom bearers, which is a blessing for all. At times, darker feelings will be part of the soul-healing journey for us as individuals and in our collective. It requires a strong and compassionate will to honour all that you feel without denying the potential wisdom of our darker emotions and also deciding to gently, but firmly, bring yourself back into communion with the sacred well of peace and delight, within. Be real, but also remember, you are of the light.

67 The Return

If you or a beloved have suffered from any kind of anguish, anything that has drained your spiritual strength and diminished your capacity to feel inherent joy, this oracle brings you glad tidings. Your ability to experience lightness of heart shall return. Take some precious time to reconnect with your heart and to your inner nature, the unlimited true self within that is not bound by personality, or external conditions. It is there within you, always. Breathe in and experience this reconnection to your true nature and know the comfort of peace. In whatever way you have veered off course, a return to your true path and a continuation of your journey from an inner place of strength, is predicted.

68

Inner Retreat for Strength

When certain situations or thoughts cast you into anxiety or fear, threatening to steal your peace of mind, it is time to reinforce your inherent spiritual right to be alive. Take your journey according to your own soul path and be free from the potential interference of negative forces. You have the right to close the door to inner patterns and outer behaviours that try to undermine your freewill. The protection of the Universal Mother is absolute. The purity of her heart, willingness to forgive and to bless, raises her to a level of empowered love that cannot be overcome by any force. Hers is an inextinguishable light, dwelling within your heart. Go to her. Already she is reaching for you from within your own heart. The power to overcome any negativity shall be granted to you.

69

Empty Force

There is something that you want to attain and a situation that you would like to heal. There is a way to accomplish this that will evoke minimal resistance and help you attract what you want rather than having to carve it out solely through your blood, sweat and tears. You can choose to push, pull and direct, but the way will be more difficult. This oracle instead suggests that you choose to set your intention, and then align and allow for circumstances to unfold. This way requires faith, flexibility and surrendering attachment to how the outcome manifests, and when. It may seem like you are giving up, but you are not. You are giving in to a greater wisdom that the manifestation you seek can happen in the strongest, most enjoyable and constructive way. Believe that things can, and will, change for the better.

70

Comparison Creates Confusion

The soul is a genius for knowing what experiences will best, and most lovingly, serve each individual being over the journey of countless lifetimes. What suits one perfectly may be a disruptive distraction for another. There is little wisdom gleaned from comparison. It tends to create envy, fear and confusion. You, and those around you, are living the life that is best suited to the needs of the soul. You don't have to understand it. You can still do what your inspired heart encourages you to do to lessen the suffering on this planet. Accept that each being is taking a unique journey, fulfilling an inner plan according to their life lessons and spiritual capacity. Know that you are making progress. Once, you likely dreamed of having what you now have in your life. In time, what you dream of now shall have manifested, too. Let your journey be as it will be.

71

Trust the Twists

To the logical mind, the next step toward success is usually obvious, if not always easy. Yet how often does life follow with opinions on how and when things should happen? The Universe sees things from a greater perspective, which enables awareness of possible obstacles, as well as ways to avoid them. It ensures inevitable success of the soul's higher purpose. Sometimes the apparent logical path could actually derail our purpose rather than support it. The Universe is not interested in 'any means to an end'. The journey itself is part of the spiritual process and designed to distil the beauty of the soul, gifting it with all that it needs. When something enters your field from left of centre, you can be sure that the greater wisdom of the Universe is at play. Let things fall apart if need be, so they can be reassembled by a loving divine hand.

72

Unique

With confidence and trust in yourself, you can choose to be the most original, authentic, creative expression of all that you are and all that you are becoming. This means giving yourself permission to rebel against the voices of fear, criticism, doubt and conformity - whether within your own head or around you. You can choose to live according to the inner values of your heart and soul. The world needs people who are willing to live from a deeply heartfelt, soul-connected place of authentic being. They have the courage to take the path of integrity, eschewing mainstream values that do not honour the human spirit and undermine dignity, grace and love. Such people become the sources of comfort and light for souls in need. You have it within you to be such a light. Don't be afraid to be different or to take what at first may seem to be a more difficult or narrower path. You have the wisdom within to know the right path for you, and the courage and consciousness to live it gleefully.

73

Beautiful Messiness

The sacred rebel within your heart does not want to be constrained by what has been, nor by the fear of making mistakes. That vital part of you wants to live, even when that entails some temporary mess as you open up to the unfamiliar. Living in integrity with your heart, even when that means life becomes more complicated or confusing for a time, will ensure that you remain true to yourself and your higher purpose. Give yourself the chance to figure your life out as you go, one step at a time. You do not need to always 'get it right' the first time. Know that things will work out anyway. There may be mess that you want to clean up, and you will, but there's a time for that. Until you sense that time is upon you, let things be, for something beautiful is wanting to emerge from within the disarray.

74

Your Inner Outsider

When you are living authentically, there will be times when you feel like an outsider, as if you don't belong to mainstream culture. That doesn't mean you need to shun society or that you don't belong. Modern culture needs loving outsiders who see things differently, live differently, and can come from the heart in service to love, without seeking to harm, control or convince another. Express and share your unique way and be humble and genuine as you offer your authenticity. There is a social need and collective soul hunger for such role models. Society needs to see the healthy contribution that finding our inner 'outsider' can bring into our lives and our culture. Don't be afraid to be such a person. It can allow for deeper connection, rather than perpetuate further isolation. The more you embrace your eccentric, quirky self, the more your path will open up for you with grace.

75

Authentic Soul

To live authentically is an inside job with outside effects. Internally, it requires time and attention to your body as it is a barometer of resonance, testing and sensing possible choices, and then making decisions based on your intuitive wisdom. This can take much courage, yet the result of it is that you feel connected to yourself and to the Universe. This is a deeply stabilising, satisfying and empowering way to live. On the outside, you end up spending quality time on what matters most to you, rather than on what matters least, which is extremely important if you want to live a meaningful, fulfilling life. There is a choice for you to make. Can you dare to make it a courageous, authentic choice? Your life path will flow from your heart. You do not need to mould yourself to fit in with a path that doesn't belong to you.

76 Connect to Empower

There is a genuine sense of empowerment that comes from connecting to your inner resources. This type of empowerment can never be taken away from you, become out of date or need to be upgraded to a new model! It can be healthy to enjoy what the world has to offer when it comes from a place of gratitude rather than fear, status-seeking or competitive consumerism masking feelings of inadequacy. You are one of the lucky ones, with access to your inner world. Your enjoyment of the outer world will become so much more constructive when your commitment to the health of your inner life is your priority. Give yourself some time to connect with yourself. You'll find a treasure of great value within.

77

There is More than One Way

When we make the choice to stop empowering stories of fear and hostility, we don't need to be so hard-headed about life, bulldozing through it as though the world will stop turning if we don't accomplish our tasks for the day. We might even become brave enough to drop the word 'only' from our vocabulary. Our minds will open when we no longer adhere to the notion that there is only this way to attain our dreams, or only that person can be the vehicle through which an inspiration can manifest. We would be ready to participate in the possible, rather than trying to corral the creativity of the Universe. There is something good that wants to happen. Refuse to allow your ego to dampen your optimistic spirit or block the good workings of the Universe.

78 Gather and Release

A thunderstorm is nature's way of gathering energy together so that it can be released. With a release of tension, relief and freedom swiftly follow, often with a fresh perspective and more energy to accomplish one's sacred work. Though we may be peace-loving at heart, allowing for the occasional wild storm as part of our soul journey, makes sense. We can participate in it with as much consciousness as we can muster, but we cannot control it. We can remember that it can help to bring matters to a head, that they may be dealt with and cleared away. Energy that is freed from a holding pattern can then flow into something new. The storm can be transformational and supportive of your path. Sometimes we just need to remember that there cannot be rainbows without a little rain. Trust that once this storm clears, a refreshing clarity shall emerge within you and a beautiful calm shall settle into your world.

79

The Bee Priestess

Bee priestess is the guardian for daring dreamers who are willing to commit themselves to a creative vision with enough gusto and boldness that it will most certainly come to life, no matter how radical or inspired that vision may be. These are the inventive types - the radicals and rebels that accomplish important tasks to support humanity in moving forward spiritually. This oracle brings encouragement for successful manifestation - especially for intentions and ideas that seem unlikely candidates for success. When the Earth Mother lends you her support - through her sacred medicine keepers, such as the bee - you can have the confidence in completion, for whom could be a more powerful ally? Keep your frequency high and your actions grounded in the practical. Expect success.

80

Inspiratrix

To be a genuine source of spiritual inspiration in this world requires a blend of the flexible with the practical. You can manage this well, for it is part of your destiny to be such a channel. This oracle encourages you to avoid judging or dismissing your ideas. Can you recognise the inimitable signature of higher spiritual intelligence in your creative urges and inspired intentions? Act upon them with curiosity as to where they will lead, rather than avoiding from a fear of failure, fear or appearing foolish. Give the loving higher intelligence of our Universe some space to flow through you and guide you on a merry journey of strange creativity and healing delight. There is wisdom in allowing yourself to be the sacred fool, at times. Do not turn away from where you feel you need to go.

81

Against the Grain

Your most potent aspirations invert the power-driven priorities of mainstream culture and conjure a world of loving wisdom, peace and truly inspired creativity. Your soul is a rebel healer, yearning for a more beautiful world for all. You don't want to do this in a superficial way, but in an alchemical way, so that ugliness and suffering of ego can be transformed into fuel to strengthen the compassionate wisdom of the soul. Do not yield to the fearful-minded constraints of your spirit. Do not allow yourself to become dulled down and conditioned into playing at being something you are not. Align your outer self with your inner truth rather than the general consensus. You will attract all that is needed from your authentic being. Believe in the power of your spirit.

82 You Cannot Miss Your Destiny

You cannot miss your destiny. What is intended for you shall find a way to reach you. However, there are certain practices that you can engage in that make the sacred reconnection between your clear sense of purpose and the empowering of the Universe manifest itself more swiftly and joyfully. The right timing cannot be rushed, nor forced, yet it is possible to minimise unnecessary obstacles, clearing the way for the most effortless fulfilment available to you. To do so, connect with and trust in your own internal rhythms, for the cycles of your own soul - rest, expansion, integration and creation - are in harmony with the wisdom of life itself. For best results, listen for what is happening deep within. Summon the confidence to be guided from within. You may worry that your path is falling away but it is not. Have faith in what is emerging.

83

The Startling Liberation

Soul is an expression of the realm of Nature, and Nature loves strange beauty, creative diversity and brilliant, spontaneous evolution. Your soul is in the process of its own startling liberation - creativity that is born through a process that likely involves a helpful shock to your system. That shock may be a rattling of your beliefs about yourself and your world. This ends up being an invitation into a more beautiful viewpoint that benefits you and empowers your path for the greater good. Embrace that which appears to have entered your world entirely 'out of the blue'. Don't give your power over to any other but do allow yourself to be a little rattled from within. It will only be for a short time and it is happening because there is a bizarre, beautiful and brilliant becoming of your own wisdom that needs to happen.

84

Legacy of Light

There is a sacred inner spiritual lineage to which your soul belongs. There were those that inspired you to fulfil your being and dedicate yourself to a constructive purpose that honours your talents and capacity. They were your spiritual mothers and fathers, helping to guide you on your path. Then there are those that shall be nourished by the light that you come to embody, a beautiful offering from which future generations may derive benefit, finding their authentic paths. Your ancestral lines are not only of blood, but also of the spirit. The legacy to which you are committed at a deep level cannot be ignored without some detriment to your wellbeing. Hand over to the Universe any concerns around fulfilment of your spiritual journey and be open to guidance. There are many beings that want, and need, your soul's success.

85

Invoke the Light

There is an infinite, continuously available source of luminous grace connected to your heart. That light has the capacity to provide all manner of assistance. To not call upon it, would be akin to unnecessary starvation when a feast is being offered. There is no such thing as asking 'too much' or 'demanding too much attention' from the spiritual realms. The beings of unconditional love that seek to assist humanity cannot do so unless invited. That is the nature of freewill. It is the nature of spiritual beings that they shine graciously and provide blessing. To invoke their assistance allows for mutual fulfilment of sacred purpose. To rely on the Light to support you, you must first invite it. There is so much that the light can bring into your world that benefit you and others. Switch scarcity thinking for the joy of prosperity consciousness and watch the goodness of grace coming to life.

86

Fierce Insight

This oracle asks you to have the courage to see beyond the assumptions, expectations, tantrums or manipulations that may steal your time and attention away from what most inspires your heart. The source of such thievery may be another's ego or the workings of your own dark side. Take care not to derail your journey out of guilt, shame, unworthiness or the belief that another's needs are more important than your own authenticity. You do not need to be drawn into the dramas of others. If you become still and listen quietly to the inner wisdom, you'll see clearly and know exactly what needs to be done (and sometimes that is simply and powerfully, to hold compassion). Be okay with each human - including you - having the right to live their own life as best they can.

87 Shifting Sands

A choice that feels correct at this time is enough. As your awareness of a situation expands, so too can your understanding of how best to proceed. You don't need to decide right now upon every single matter as it pertains to the rest of your life. You have permission to change your mind if necessary, to learn from what unfolds, and adjust your course as needed. That is called being alive. "Being perfect" does not feature anywhere in that description! Sometimes as a result of a choice, certain events are set in motion and you simply cannot know what your next move will be until the dust has settled and you see the lay of the land, once more. Make your choices one by one and trust that it is okay to let your life happen. When you need to, you will know what is true and what to do.

88

Releasing Allegiances

It is time to hold yourself, and that requires letting go of another - even if just for a time. You can step away from a connection with gratitude for all that you learned and recognise its value. Recognise that although you had your learning curves, and it wasn't always easy, you conducted yourself with as much dignity and awareness as you could muster and have grown through the process. You are not the same person you were before that connection began. This is good. Your bond may be revived and restored through the spaciousness, or you may realise that a deeper letting go is required. You have the wisdom and courage you need to be discerning, but you do need time for inner reflection to do so. Solitude does not need to equate with loneliness. Diverting energy into your inner world will not hamper your outer activities - if anything it will fuel them with more vitality in the long run. Take the time to honour yourself and go within. There is no need to be afraid.

89

Light in the Darkness

The soul, in its holistic wisdom, will at times move through experiences of the darker side of life, experiencing loss, suffering and pain. Choosing to believe that there is a higher purpose behind that suffering can enhance your ability to accept and therefore move through such experiences more swiftly, gaining wisdom through the process. In deep challenge, our soul pearl is formed - this is the pearl beyond price, grown through struggle, rare and hard won. This oracle asks you to recognise that something worthy and extraordinary is developing within your soul as you move through your life. Do not give in to despair. Honour your suffering as a way to learn about yourself, but do not believe that it is reflective of the bigger picture, nor the deciding factor in your ultimate happiness. Though you likely cannot see or feel it quite at this moment, something very precious is happening within your heart. Hold tight. You will emerge from this victorious on so many levels.

90

Sabotaging the Saboteurs

Sometimes, it can be easier to notice the negativities of those around us more than the darkness within. Yet the voices of fear, anger, hate, criticism, shame, guilt and doubt that come from within - perhaps internalised from significant figures in our lives a long time ago - have the potential to undermine our growth. If we allow them to do so! There's no need to fear the negativity within, but there is a need to recognise it, calmly and firmly setting a boundary against it by choosing to affirm one's innate spiritual value. You have nothing to prove to yourself or anyone else. Stay in your heart. Be in connection with the dignity, compassion and humour within that creates a safeguard from outer and inner saboteurs. Have unwavering faith in your ultimate triumph.

91 The Unscripted Journey

The path that you now tread is a delicious confluence of divine destiny and unscripted, spontaneous life. To embrace this journey, remember that change can bring such blessings. You may be surprised at how much you can leave behind now, without feeling concerned or anxious. You will be able to travel lighter than you ever imagined. Just as the butterfly leaves the chrysalis behind when it is time to spread its newly formed wings, so too shall you be ready to leave behind what once held you within, in order to expand according to the natural evolution of your soul. The past has served a purpose. You can feel good about what has been, and about where you are heading. This oracle brings confirmation of a significant change taking place in your life, according to the inner timing and awakening of the soul. Trust in the natural timing of your own emergence.

92 Soul Turning

Whilst remaining present in the healing essence of this moment, keep your heart open to the powerful potential unfolding right now. The groundwork for future fulfilment is now being laid. Don't worry about where you may be led, or how it will play out. You don't need to foresee or to direct in order to benefit from what is happening. If it feels like nothing much is happening, then have a little patience and trust, for the subtle inner turnings of your soul are generating sacred fire. From that etheric heat, seeds of manifestation are ripening. Your soul garden shall come into full bloom. It is only a matter of time.

93

Rule Breaker

There are subtle - and sometimes not-so-subtle - pressures to adhere to convention and follow the mainstream rules about how to live, when to do certain things, and how to be normal (whatever that is). However, some souls do far better, thriving and flourishing with creative fire, when they choose to move outside of the conventional plans. There is a freedom for the fringe-dwelling soul that more conservative types cannot know. Even if your eccentric streak is hidden from the view of most people, you know that it is within you and that when you listen to it, you truly feel like you are being yourself. That is when it is easiest for the Universe to support, inspire and protect you. Do not be afraid to dispense with convention and live according to an inner sense of things. Break free.

94 Quake if You Must then Commit

Sometimes we have a vision that inspires but is so bold that it also causes us to quake in our boots! We may wonder if we have what it takes. Creatively living your light can be equal measures of terrifying and wondrous when you open up to a fearless acceptance of bigger, brighter, more radical possibilities. If you are going to be an adventurous soul committed to living your life as fully as possible, then there will be growth edges that demand breaking the mould and forging more expansive perspectives on what is possible. Remember when something is right for you, stunning synchronicities and support will flow your way, matching your every effort with glorious grace. The Universe has lovingly thrown down the gauntlet. The knowledge that nothing shall defeat you will empower you to pick it up and run with it. Cultivate self-assurance. You've got this.

95 Pleasure of Passionate Purpose

To feel called to a higher purpose and go through the inner healing journey required to actualise that calling, is a way to give something back to the giver of precious life. The genuine desires of the heart are the sacred urgings of the Universe, rich with potential for nourishing pleasure. If you have been shamed or judged, made to feel guilt, or denied your natural desires and pleasures, you may have developed a complicated, or even confused, connection to the yearnings of your heart. If you come to understand what your innermost desires are really communicating to you, then channel your passionate energies into fuelling your will and commit to a purpose that enriches your life. In doing so, you gain the capacity to enrich the lives of others, too. Allow yourself some authentic pleasure. Let your path be one not only of discipline but also of delight.

96 There is no Substitute for the Sacred

Trust in what you truly want. Not the substitutions, nor the 'make dos', but in that which would truly generate a sense of meaning and fulfilment in your life. You don't need a detailed grand plan. Start with what you know. Perhaps it is that you yearn to write, sing, dance, garden or learn how to meditate, start a business or adopt a child, or engage in some sort of training. Your commitment to each step, as it becomes clear to you, sets sacred manifestation in motion. Every step evokes the responsiveness of the wild and graceful Universe in your life. Don't play it safe. Go for what you want.

97

Magic in Her Method

The sacred feminine, the goddess, is a supreme creatrix, capable of beautifully timed manifestations according to higher workings of wisdom and generous good-natured genius. As she works in spirals, rather than in a linear way, there can be moments in our creative manifestation process where we might feel that we are farther away than ever from what we are seeking. Yet in a short time, we will suddenly find ourselves in the right place, at the right moment, and seemingly out of nowhere things fall into place. Do not give in to the voices of doom and gloom that say it 'should have happened by now so it won't happen at all'. Fortunately, the marvellous methods of the goddess cannot be constrained by the fearful predictions of humankind. Trust in her wild ways.

98

Urge to Create

The compulsion to unbind your heart, body and mind from ego drama and bring forth the inner treasures of peace, comfort, inspiration, courage and optimism is a true urging of the soul. If there is something happening in your life that you consider is beyond healing, hand it over to the Universe, knowing that the Universe has the means and willingness to reshape all matters to a far more pleasing form, for all. You will be surprised at what you see manifesting when you least expect it. Trust in that inner urge to bring through that which is new, improved and more loving. It is not your imagination working overtime. It is a recognition of something beautiful that wants to be birthed.

99

Ascending Gracefully

Do you believe that you have to claw your way to the top of your particular mountain to obtain what you desire? Could there be a more co-operative, creative approach where you don't have to push quite so hard to receive what is naturally coming? When the 'push' comes from a place of uncertainty, it is time to relax and cultivate a little more faith in yourself and the Universe. All things come in time, rightfully and according to a loving wisdom. We cannot know the intricate workings of divine timing and how the destinies of all beings are intertwined, but we can know that we are part of it, and be a little more trusting, a little more curious, a little more optimistic about what is and what shall be. Your spirit is rising. Recognise this and your mind can let go with peacefulness and trust.

100

Mind Games

The mind conjures up possible problems and dwells upon them as probabilities or even inevitabilities. The heart, feeling for the truths beneath the 'what ifs' of the mind, approaches life differently. The heart lives in intimate conversation with what is happening in our lives - from the moments that feel like sheer sublime grace to the moments that have us feeling challenged, confused and conflicted. The heart can do this because it has a capacity that the mind does not - the ability to trust in the face of mystery. Giving credence to mind games will not contribute positively to your life experience. Better to trust the heart. Whatever it is that makes no sense at the moment shall eventually be recognised as being incredibly helpful, and a way onto a path that you most certainly wish to be on.

101

The Long Term

We can gain insight from what has happened in the past, but we cannot live there. Nor can we live well if we attempt to 'live for the future', directing all of our energies toward what may happen. We need to be here and now, to find fulfilment and participate in the mystery of our lives. This oracle asks you to ground yourself in this moment. Even if you do not consciously recognise it at this time, whatever is happening will prove to be beneficial in the long term. So, let yourself simply be here, and yet ... also be hopeful for what is to be!

102

Potential of a Seedling

It can be all too easy to dismiss the smaller steps that we might take as insignificant. Perhaps even to the point of wondering whether we should bother making the effort. If you are dreaming of accomplishing great things, then at times you may feel overwhelmed by just how much needs to be done to manifest your dream. In such moments, you need to take special care of your visionary heart. That care includes not allowing negativity or defeatism to gain a stronghold within. It also requires that you not become overly ambitious for what can be accomplished in a day, nor dismiss just how much can take place in an hour of committed work or a second of spiritual communion. Honour your spiritual promises to yourself. Do not underestimate the cumulative power of small steps toward manifestation. Allow progress, rather than perfection, to be enough. All things will come together, not necessarily according to your preferred timing, but in such a way that you - and many others - will benefit bliss.

103

Hold Your Course

Developing the capacity to surrender, to become flexible, to attune and respond to life's currents is how we co-create with the Universe. However, there are times when we need to stay true to a particular path, even if it feels like the sands are shifting from beneath our feet. Sometimes certain elements within our world, and within our own minds, need to give way for a greater manifestation to happen. A bumpy road is not necessarily an indicator that it is the wrong road to be on. Sometimes we need to stand our ground whilst chaos washes through our lives, trusting that there is a good-intentioned, higher purpose to what is happening, and everything will eventually fall into place. At times, the soul has need of sacred stubbornness. It is not holding out against the workings of life. It is rather demonstrating the grit and inner strength required to grow. You have the determination to see this through.

104 Vulnerability is a Sign of Growth

In every birth, at the opening of a new cycle in our lives, there is a natural and appropriate vulnerability. At this time, new life is emerging from the depths of your soul, like a fresh green shoot rising up from the earth. This newness, as fragile or insignificant or vulnerable as it may seem, matters greatly. Steady yourself against carelessness, dismissiveness and negativity, as well as overly inflated demands or controlling projections about what it must become. This new energy within simply needs to be protected and allowed to grow into what it is. That may entail keeping your own counsel, with a shroud of sacredness and privacy around what needs time to develop before it becomes strong enough to stand on its own, unfazed by the responses of the outer world.

105

A Room of Your Own

A room of your own refers to an inner sanctuary of your spirit, kept pure. You might have a particular place where you go to meditate, pray or relax in order to enter into that inner room. From time to time, you'll notice that others have taken up residence in the inner temple of your heart, demanding attention or causing you to ruminate upon their problems. That is not the rightful place for them to be. This room is your own and needs tending so that it is clear and radiant with spaciousness, compassion and purity. Then it can regularly refresh your spirit, providing you with an abundance of inner resources to support you in living and loving well. Firmly clear out intrusions from your inner space and take sanctuary in the openness and beauty of the radiance within.

106 One Step Ahead is Plenty

If we attempt to venture too far ahead, we may abandon a marvellous plan because we cannot see how it could become a success. Yet perhaps only a few more steps, and suddenly a pathway would have become clear and our faith in the process so much easier! We have to give the Universe a little faith so that it can work its healing magic in our lives. You can be a radical optimist (which I highly encourage) and believe that everything will work out. You just need to realise that most of the time, if you are co-creating something with the Universe, then you'll not have any clue how it's going to work out. Pull your mind back a little so that you don't fret and withdraw from a truly inspired undertaking. With your continued participation, the genius of the Universe is going to weave everything together.

107

Life is Wild and Wise

There are times when an inner compulsion to do something erupts from within. You may not know exactly what it is that you are meant to do, but you know that until you act, a part of you simply cannot rest. Be with the tension of knowing that there is an action for you to take and that there is a lack of clarity around what that might be. As you sit quietly in that place of inner tension and ask the Universe to show you the way of wisdom, you will sense what and when it is needed. You'll eventually be taking the step instinctively, and most likely only realising that you are doing so whilst you are in the process. That's how natural and in-the-moment your action will be. Trust in the wisdom of life and your own capacity to be in alignment with it.

108

Nourished Soul

The weight of habitual, often negative, thought can make it difficult for the soul to truly recognise and be nourished by the unconditional love of spirit. Instead of an open channel flowing between your soul and spirit, the obstructive fabrications of ego are trampling on your peace of mind and clamouring for your attention. The soul then feels lacking in its natural joy, optimism and sense of inner freedom. Clearing the inner channel regularly allows spirit to infuse the soul and keep it attuned to what is real - which has nothing to do with the endless judgements and opinions generated by the ego. Still the worrisome mind by giving yourself permission to not need to know how everything is going to unfold and yet trust that the Universe is on your side and everything is going to be okay. Choose some emotional and mental spaciousness. Let spirit - and the joyful peace and optimism it brings - make a connection with your heart. Choose to believe beneath all that is happening, or apparently not happening, all is well.

109 From Tension to Breakthrough

The nature of the heart is such that within its fulfilment is the promise of fulfilment for all beings. In devoting yourself to the path of your heart, you are contributing to the collective in more ways that you can possibly know. There are times when our networks of sacred connection need strengthening, to remind the soul that it is not alone. The spirit can sense this, translating it as an urge to co-operate and co-create with conscious, like-minded souls, toward a greater purpose. This can entail friction as different approaches or ideas clash for a time. That friction can turn up the heat, which is needed to stimulate the creative seeds and ensure ripening. Do not turn away from this tension. Nor hold yourself hostage to it. Instead, be part of the process. Be true to yourself as you take the healing and helpful path of collaborative creativity, allowing it to bring out the best in you. You will be able to balance the needs of your own heart with the needs of those around you. You have more skilfulness here than you realise.

110

Future Human

Humanity is evolving. The future human is growing out of the spiritual ground currently being tended by highly individualistic, creative soul types who live in harmony with a loving inner connection to their own journey of healing and awakening. The founding spiritual fathers and mothers of the evolving human collective need a strong sense of self in order to engage actively with others, without losing one's own voice. Such souls need to remember to stay true to their own work, recognising that this doesn't have to separate them from others. Rather, it strengthens the clarity and helpfulness of what they can offer. Continue to develop yourself and in doing so, you shall be assisting those around you, as they benefit from your increasing spiritual maturity. Nurture your hopeful heart and continue to contribute positively toward what can be for our future generations of humans.

111 Truth Behind the Images

Sometimes we believe what others tell us we are, as though the self we see reflected through their eyes is somehow more compelling than what we know our own selves to be. Yet the accuracy of a reflection depends on the clarity of that which is doing the reflecting. Even the moon can only reflect the sun in varying degrees of faithfulness. It is not a matter of ill will; it is the mechanics of the situation. Take care that you don't allow the images others form of you to interfere with you learning how to know, validate and believe in yourself. To attempt to see a full sun in the partiality of the moon doesn't lead to clarity. Turn your gaze inwards and seek direct experience of your true nature. There you will find steadying reassurance and peaceful strength.

112

Breaking Contracts

Negative experiences can be responded to in such a way that they become fuel for strengthening our wisdom, boundaries, compassion and our determination to continue. However, this doesn't mean that one needs to allow for continuing negativity. Give yourself internal permission to spiritually break with unconscious agreements that you have made with others, in particular any person that you have given power to determine your value as a human or to bully you to go against your own truth. You matter enough to have been given the precious gift of Life. You have the right to live as you so choose.

113

After the Storm

You are not forgotten. You have not been overlooked or denied. Nor have you been assessed and found to be wanting or rejected as unworthy. There is a storm that needs to be unleashed within your heart. It is not to cause drama for you or another. It is to free your heart from the stories of the past. Sometimes old traumas just need physical release in order to be laid to rest. So, allow your soul a sacred rain dance. Release any gathered energy and inner holding on by expressing whatever emotion, prayer, wordless sounds or authentic movements you feel. Then you shall be in alignment with the powerful healing wisdom of your life path, and in harmony with the sweet plan that the Universe holds for you. The storm shall erupt and so it should, for afterwards there is the needed relief of cleansing and renewed readiness to receive.

114 You Know So Let Go

Like the ancient forests, spiralling galaxies and the astonishing caterpillar-to-butterfly process, there is a natural intelligence for growth that is beyond logic. We are governed by an intelligent force so powerful it literally shapes our world. It is so invisible that we forget its presence and become anxious to figure out how everything must happen, and when. This intelligence is within you. You know how to grow without knowing how you know. The answers you need are a lot closer than you realise, and a lot easier to implement than your fear would have you believe. Relax, lean into your process, and trust yourself.

115 Positive Progress

Even if you can see no sign to justify hope, this oracle confirms that you are making positive progress and a breakthrough is imminent. Remember that so much is happening when the seed is still unbroken in the ground. Below the earth, encased in its protective shell, it is summoning up all the might, power and strength it needs to crack through the outer layers, and push both down into the soil and up toward the light. It is essential that this process happens before anything else can take place. Yet all of that essential brilliance and incredibly strength happens unseen. We have to trust that our efforts are enough and continue to apply ourselves, knowing that when the timing is right, emergence will occur. The beautiful evidence of your efforts will come to light. Continue to apply yourself to the tasks at hand.

116 Helping Hand from the Universe

What a human can accomplish through one's own efforts can be extraordinary. However, when embarking on a spiritual path, there will be times when what is necessary for fulfilment is rather more than one person can accomplish through willpower alone. Certain situations require spiritual intervention to set events right. When you recognise such a need for grace in your life and in the world, then your prayers and yearnings can be the catalyst for spiritual alchemy, triggering a series of uplifting twists that could not have otherwise occurred. Spirit is very powerful, but it cannot intervene for betterment of our affairs unless a human being uses their freewill to invite it to do so. Let your willpower be supplemented by the spiritual workings of a greater intelligence at play. For you, and for all, ask for divine blessing and assistance for the greater good. There is something beautiful that spirit wants to happen, for you.

117 Empowering Spiritual Grace Through Faith

I invite you to empower spiritual grace in your life through this affirmation of love, light and wisdom. If you wish to enact this, open your heart to the words, as if your soul is speaking to the Universe. Listen deeply or even choose to speak them aloud: "I ask for all disappointments that have led me to believe life is not trustworthy or that faith is not reliable, be released from my body, mind and soul. I ask for support to accept that I can and will attract all that I need into my life, in perfect time and in the perfect way. Having faith in spirit will help all beings increase the presence of grace in this world. May the light shine bright for the greatest good of all."

118

Spiritual Gift

There is a loving sweetness seeking to find its way into your heart and world in the form of a spiritual gift. This spiritual gift may be symbolic, something that might not seem like a big deal, yet in your heart you recognise it as being sacred and meaningful. It is not the form of the gift - whether a physical object or an inner vision - that holds the power. That is just the wrapping. The actual gift itself is a subtle yet effective empowerment, a spiritual booster shot that helps you move forward with greater clarity and joy in your step. Whether an obvious windfall or a more subtle jolt of energy that nonetheless uproots a previously entrenched problem, you shall experience the workings of grace when you most need them.

119

Breaking Down Walls

Before a new way can emerge, the old way must be dismantled. This naturally occurs when the soul has outgrown certain identities or defences, and even belief systems that might have once been considered essential to your journey. Sometimes, outer appearances and forms become too constricting for the truth of your being and they begin to crumble as you expand. Sometimes internal beliefs fail you, because there is a more encompassing, generous belief that better supports your journey. At times, you may find the process painful. Keep your eye on the spiritual prize and you'll recognise the workings of grace helping you feel trust and relief as you let go in order to be built up anew.

120

Wordless Truth

Truth always speaks to us, but not always in words. It may communicate through a feeling that brings about an inexplicable sense that everything is going to work out perfectly, even if we don't know how. This oracle confirms that you are hearing an unspoken truth, and it is wise to acknowledge that, even if it seems like no-one else around you can recognise it. Hold your truth with compassion. Resist using it like a knife to cut yourself, or another, with harshness. Instead, allow it to be the clear insight that allows you to loosen internal knots and unbind your soul from confusion. What you need to know will come to you and you will have the wisdom to recognise it when it does.

121

Overcoming Ill Will

The ego is a disruptive force. Unlike the divine disruption of the soul that breaks down negative patterns, the disruption of the ego seeks to undermine what is constructive. If you have been worn down by the antics of ego, disheartened by mean-spirited gossip or those that seem intent on purposefully blocking your path, do not fret. Disconnect from negative sources and commune with the infinite through sacred pursuits such as contemplation of nature, snort laughing whenever possible and heartfelt meditation. If that ill will has somehow penetrated your heart or mind, connecting with sources of light will cleanse you from the inside and restore you back to your authentic, peaceful nature. What is meant to be is spiritually protected. That includes the sanctity of your own heart. Immerse your attention in your sacred realm and leave the workings of ego to their own fate.

122

Gathering of the Light

Spiritual light is gathering around you, attracted to the purity of your heart. To enhance this light, don't identify with it or try to claim it as your own. Simply acknowledge it as luminous presence flowing through a pure heart, touching the world. In the sanctity of this light, a pathway is cleared, strengthened and protected. There is magic that wants to happen! Stay true to your path, don't become distracted by what others are doing, nor dilute your energy by attempting to pursue too much all at once. Continue to commit and build, whilst remaining consciously connected to the gathering light within. You are so close to succeeding. Stay focused.

123

Spiritual Rescue

Your soul is in need of spiritual rescue, deep rest, a reset and revitalisation. You work hard and have accomplished much already, yet you can often pass over your accomplishments too swiftly, focusing immediately on the next step. Your dedication is admirable. However, you need to put down the pen, paintbrush, or cookbook sometimes and take time out to experience the connection to your body, breath, nature and the infinite spirit. Restoration does not always have to be a long and involved process. Even a relatively brief time of switching gears can have a powerful tonic effect on the soul. You will then feel like you are yourself again and return to life with renewed vigour and clarity. Take some time to give back to yourself.

124 The Value of In-Between-Ness

This oracle confirms that you are in a phase of transition between one level of experience and an evolutionary shift onto new spiritual ground. If you are struggling to break free, feeling as though you are caught in a repetitive loop, consider reframing your perspective. Let the situation be an opportunity to look at old patterns in a new way, from a stronger and wiser vantage point that considers the growth you have accomplished already. Give yourself credit for how much you've grown. If you have been wondering if a new cycle can open up for you, this oracle brings confirmation. Take steps toward new endeavours and projects that resonate with your heart, as they can assist you in successfully transitioning to the next level of fulfilment.

125 Soul Mothering

The capacity for soul mothering is not limited to bearing or raising children, although it can certainly include that experience. It also includes working with grown individuals or collectives in such a way that they are supported to mature spiritually. They may need your devotion and energy, your belief in their value, and your willingness to be the protective, fierce mother tigress, or the supportive shoulder to lean upon, so that their higher purpose may be sheltered from ego and encouraged to flourish. This oracle acknowledges your capacity to support and love those around you in a healthy way. It asks you to allow yourself to feel supported, loved and nurtured, too. There is also a special message here about healing childhood issues that is allowing for a new way to live and be to emerge.

126

Love Freely

You are invited to love freely and tremendously, at a deeper level, with generosity and without conditions. This love can be shared with yourself and others. You can do this as you let go of what you have been taught about love, and instead allow love itself to be your teacher and guide. This invitation can manifest itself in numerous ways - through a personal connection with another human being, a deeper awakening to the love of the planet and her creatures, or to your own body, as a beautiful animal devoted to your spirit. As you settle into the experience of loving connectedness, you can let go of aloneness in favour of oneness and be restored. Let your heart love. It will bring you such healing and empower your journey in ways you cannot yet foresee.

127

Sacred Fool

The sacred fool is able to subvert ego paradigms and proceed outside of conventional restraints that try to control how things should be done. He holds spiritual genius in his soul. He lives according to an inner prompting, and cares not for whether others see the wisdom in his method, or madness. This oracle heralds a time when you will feel that the only way to step forward on your life path is to do so in a way that embraces something that might seem a bit crazy to the logic-lovers amongst your tribe. Break with your own self-imposed conventions, because they are too small to allow for the adventure that is calling you onwards. Go with it, without needing to understand the divine mind that inspires it. Let yourself be the one who is becoming sane through recognising the insanity of the world and refusing to bow down to it.

128 Your Sacred Work

Dreamer of beautiful dreams, bring your visions to life. The world needs not only your dreams, but your creations. Get thee to thy desk! Thy easel! Thy computer! Work, beloved. Don't just dream, create! This oracle reinforces the value of your sacred work - whatever it is that moves you from the depths of your heart. Forget about social conventions. Don't be held back from whether or not something seems practical. The Universe loves a bold spirit. With each step you take, it rushes toward you like a chivalrous lover opening doors, hand gently on your back, or tugging at your hair enthusiastically, all in order to guide you. You will be provided with what is needed to take another step. And another. And then another. Do your part. This oracle augurs all manner of assistance to ensure the best outcome.

129 The Real You Thrives in Secret

If you experienced controlling and manipulative forces, rather than unconditional welcome whilst growing up, you may find it difficult to access your real self. That self will be hidden away, deep within, as a form of protection from an unsafe world. You now have the opportunity to let go of who you were taught to be, in order to become who you really are. You are enough of a badass to build yourself up from within, not allowing the outer world to decide your worth for you. Layers of shame from early conditioning can be difficult to experience, but as they dissolve, your true self is revealed beneath them. The courageous and divinely defiant self declares, "I am going to love myself anyway!" This will allow the real you to breathe and be free. This oracle says you are powerful enough to break the cycle of shaming. It is time to stop the shame and claim yourself lovingly, instead. Then the real you can thrive openly.

130

Right to the Light

When moving through the darkness of our suffering, there will be times when we feel disconnected from the love and peace within. It is in those moments that we need to remember our right to the light. When we are in the midst of suffering, this inner access to spiritual presence is available to us always, no matter how disconnected we feel from all things spiritual. The right to light means that it is always there for us, and we have the right to call upon spiritual grace at all times and for all things. We are encouraged to exercise that right. It is capable of reaching us in any state of mind, in any place and at any time, bringing relief. Even now, it is tapping at the door to your heart. Open to it.

131

It Will Happen

Even the most dedicated creative spirit can go through phases of feeling as if they are going through the motions, but not gaining any traction or movement on their path. Sometimes there is a willingness and desire to take action and get things moving, but no opportunities to do so on the horizon. This oracle brings you a message of hope. Beneath the experience of stagnancy, a change is brewing. Inner workings will continue to gather momentum and eventually surge with sufficient power to open up a way through. The dissatisfied mind shall be placated by the magnitude of what is happening. It will take continued commitment, but the holding pattern shall give way for a more expansive reality. Do not abandon ship! Wait - and you shall see.

132

No Harm Shall Befall You

Whatever has been bothering you will not be able to harm you. You will prevail. If you are concerned that someone or something is 'getting away with something' or blocking your path, or causing harm to a loved one, place your trust in the Universe. Ask for divine protection for the good of all, and know that all prayers are answered with justice, mercy and wisdom. In shifting the way that you are looking at this situation - perhaps seeking where you might distil even a tiny morsel of healing insight for yourself - the energy in what is beheld begins to shift. There is no need to fear. Resolution is on its way and you are spiritually protected.

133

Restless for Rebirth

Do you ever feel like you want something, but you cannot quite articulate what that something is? Those are the times when growth simply must happen. Restlessness, excitement, or even anxiety as you feel compelled toward an unknown future, may be part of your experience of growth. Negative responses toward what is happening are not an accurate assessment of what is unfolding for you. They are an accurate indication of emotional distress, likely sourced from childhood, which requires a response of compassion, rather than panic. In whatever ways work for you, connect with the sources of spiritual light that you love the most. Relax into their comfort and assistance. You will know when to act, what to do, and when to let things unfold. Let your restlessness move you further along your inner journey without becoming impatient or forceful in your approach. As you grow, your outlook will become considerably more positive.

134 Listen for the Quiet Voice Within

Oftentimes, the clearest and truest guidance is not the loudest voice within. Fear and doubt can yell, where love and trust speak quietly and consistently from deep within the heart. This oracle guides you to trust in the quiet truths of the heart, even when the voices of fear within you or around you may appear to be more powerful. The truths of the heart cut through mental anguish. We can recognise the simple truths of the heart in our bones. We may know that we need to act when we would rather not, or wait, when we would rather act. Yet when we rest into the heart with trust, our capacity and courage rise to meet the task. Tune into your heart. Know that you shall be fine.

135

Beautiful Becoming

There is so much more to you than meets the eye. There are aspects of your authentic self that you are yet to discover, let alone share with others. The Universe knows you and your best path, to manifest your innate potential. You are asked to gather faith within your heart so that your fulfilment becomes inevitable in your own mind, rather than a hopeful fantasy. The Universe is on side with your fulfilment. Even a 'no' is a hidden 'yes', from a higher perspective. No-one else can live your destiny and you are being helped by a most powerful ally for your success.

136

Ripening

The time for harvest has come. This oracle augurs readiness. Yes, there is more 'becoming' ahead of you. Yes, there are further accomplishments that you shall manifest. There is a blessing for future success, and there is empowerment to step forward on your path now. Something has matured and become ready to be shared. Do not turn away, do not hide, do not underestimate yourself, or the power of divine timing. If you have often pushed forward, but felt held back, it may be less familiar for you to sense hesitancy within yourself when the way before you is finally clear and ready. Step forward anyway. This is your time.

137 No Good Thing Shall be Withheld

Confidence is especially important on the spiritual path. Confidence that the Universe loves you and knows what it is doing, and confidence that when the Universe sends the unexpected your way, you'll rally and deal with it. Confidence allows you to make your choices from a place of love rather than fear. Fear-based decisions promise relief but actually tend to create even more problems. This oracle suggests that you acknowledge aloud whatever problem needs solving, and then create a little inner spaciousness, based on a relaxed and trusting attitude of confidence, so that the Universe can, and will, step in to sort things out. Joyfully anticipate an abundance of blessings made manifest in your world.

138

Emotional Skilfulness

The soul needs authentic experience to grow. The more difficult emotions of anger, grief, sadness, loneliness and fear, can be part of how the courageous soul experiences healing that leads to wisdom. When we trust in the healing journey, we recognise that it will draw to us whatever it is that we need, even if we cannot always understand how some particularly painful situation could be helpful. If we choose to trust anyway, we will move through the experience, gaining something of value, such as reclaiming a part of your own precious soul. Reflect on your emotions and consider the deeper meaning of what you feel, but do not let them consume your heart and mind. Once you process what you are feeling, your perspective shall lighten up considerably and your trust in the goodness of the Universe will be fully restored.

139

The Dark Goddess

The goddess loves all creatures unconditionally, and continuously. In her light aspect of peace and tenderness, this is easier to acknowledge than when she is in her dark aspect of ferocious compassion and sacred wrath. She may manifest her wisdom, leading us into direct confrontation with the very things we want to avoid. Although it may feel as though life has turned against us in such moments, her dark workings do have a luminous purpose. As we move through the experience, we become more spiritually empowered, able to transform negativity - through healing - into positive energy. We don't waste energy jumping through quite so many hoops to avoid pain. We become more willing to trust her hand at work in our lives, and therefore feel less afraid. We become more capable of truly living and through this, fulfilling our sacred destiny. Rally your courage, deal with the darkness, but keep your optimism in full force. Things are going to work out.

140 The Universe Wants to Help

Being honest with yourself about your suffering is an act of wisdom. It doesn't mean you are weak, or insufficiently enlightened, or that you (or anyone else) has to become a martyr to your suffering. When you acknowledge something isn't right in your world, you set a healing process in motion. The Universe is not sitting idly by, twiddling its massive cosmic thumbs, entertained by our struggles. It is a loving, interactive, responsive and intelligent presence that holds the space for our suffering with tremendous compassion, gentleness and peacefulness, whilst raging and aching along with us. It is ready to leap forth with bold and helpful inventiveness the moment we are open to receive spiritual intervention. There is no judgement of your suffering. There is only goodwill and skilfulness that wish to flow toward you, showing you the way beyond suffering. Be with what you feel for as long as you need while remaining firm in your faith that it can and will heal, as soon as you are ready.

141

Go to the Meeting Point

If you can acknowledge rather than hide from what you are struggling with, you open up a divine dialogue, a cosmic connection, and an outpouring of responsive grace. You create a meeting point for you and the divine. You acknowledge the problem and hold patient, trusting space for resolution. Sometimes it takes a while to recognise the goodness of spiritual intervention at work in our lives. It is powerfully effective but often subtle to the point of being invisible. The best we can usually hope for is a brief whiff of its sweet fragrance in the divine aftermath of resolution. You can tell that it worked wonders because of what has happened, but you couldn't explain how or when all that wondrousness took place. The message from this oracle is to talk to the Universe about what is bothering you with the expectation of a positive and helpful response.

142

Protective Prayerfulness

Prayer is a powerful practice. There is no need to worry about saying the right words, coming up with a special formula, or needing to have a certain set of beliefs to comply with others. To pray, you simply speak from the heart and ask the divine - whatever you conceive this to be - for assistance. This oracle encourages you to pray at this time. You may not know what you are supposed to pray for, but the act of prayer itself is what will serve you now and is even more important than what you are praying for (a prayer that all beings receive the help they need, when they need it, is always a good prayer). The act of prayer forces you to make contact with your own inner being. The spiritual field generated by your prayer will protect you from distortions and distractions, keeping you connected to your true path and personhood. It also helps every other being through that increased spiritual presence. You have more spiritual influence than you realise. Don't be afraid to put it to its best use!

143 Let Go of What No Longer Serves

It can be surprising how much of what lies between dissatisfaction and the fulfilment of our heart is of our own creation. We often focus on outer issues - timing and other people supporting us or invalidating us, as being the major roadblocks on our path. Such matters can be relevant, but they are not in our personal realm of control. Our power to evoke positive changes lies in meeting the inner obstacles. They can include beliefs about lack of worthiness and capability, fear of being ridiculed and shamed, rejection for being our true, weirdly wonderful self. It can be hard to let go of the walls we have built against the very thing that we want, because to do so requires that our innermost fears be acknowledged. We might feel vulnerable, yet there is power in our vulnerability. In its realness and honesty, it attracts solutions. Let your attachment to the past be overcome by your optimism for the beauty of what can be.

144 Higher Purpose is Protected

Your sacred higher purpose is to become what you are - which is why no-one can steal your purpose, nor live your life for you. Each of us needs to find our way home spiritually, to connect with the heart, and to liberate our passion for living our particular life path to the full. It matters not whether our path seems ordinary or spiritual. There can be unnecessary pressure to translate your higher purpose into a job. It is wonderful to seek work that inspires you and utilises your talents fully. However, living your life is your ultimate higher purpose. As you choose to live your life in a way that you grow as a human being - becoming stronger, kinder and more loving - you are fulfilling your most sacred destiny. As like attracts like, it is also the way to draw more opportunities for sacred, authentic self-expression into your world. So just be you, as best and as brightly as you can.

145

You Get to Choose

You have the choice to respond to whatever is directed your way. You may welcome it, accept it, set a boundary around yourself or acknowledge that it has no place in your heart. You have much power in you - the power of how to respond. Your choice is like a stone tossed into a lake, generating ripples of effect. Your consciously chosen action interacts with what is, creatively igniting change. You don't have to control or contrive your responses so much as reflect and be authentic in your response. To sense the full gamut of authentic responses available to you - including those of a game-changing higher vibrational level - you may need to surrender the situation temporarily. In creating a little space where you ask for a higher wisdom to inform your actions, a higher perspective can inspire your response. You have the spiritual wherewithal to proceed in such a way that your actions will be able to find and affirm the positive in a negative situation.

146

Motherly Miracles

Our Universal Mother loves all beings and wishes to assist, support and encourage your spiritual evolution. To this end, her grace flows generously, and an intention of that grace is to integrate your spiritual journey in your physical life experience. Her creative blessing constantly unfolds through our lives, weaving synchronicity and intelligent responsiveness. So vast is the scale of creative unfoldment that our mind would easily become overwhelmed by what is essentially unfathomable to anything other than the trusting heart that needs no explanation. In terms of the grand scheme of your life path, it is actually better not to try to know it all right now, but to work with what you can know and do in the now, trusting the Universal Mother's enormous capacity for multi-tasking to manage all the rest.

147

Courage for the Task

To fulfil the sacred destiny of your own spiritual path, you'll need courage. Courage will help you trust your heart as you sense each task before you, and then have the spiritual fortitude to accomplish it. Whether seemingly small and insignificant steps or more demanding tasks, courage is required to act with faith, especially if those tasks lead you into situations where you could be triggered emotionally. Of course, you can trust the task is meant to help you heal that particular wound. It can be difficult to help someone who won't help themselves. When we do what we can to live with courage, we empower the flow of grace in our lives, from the many spiritual beings that are seeking to assist us. This oracle speaks of a blessing. Take your step and the Universe shall rally to support your healing and spiritual destiny.

148 From Prayer to Peaceful Change

Sometimes we are tired from the fight and the struggle, and the thought of yet more hard work ahead evokes a sense of despair. For some who believe that they must be the warrior, constantly fighting, such moments are likely to be the only time they truly let go in prayerful surrender and allow spiritual assistance to enter their hearts. Perhaps you are one such soul, or you may have simply been praying for help, or wondering if you should pray for help, on a matter of concern. This oracle foretells a peaceful change will come from surrendering through prayer.

149 Change can Happen with Grace

Not all change - even dramatic change - has to be quite so difficult. Sometimes the thought of change might be frightening, at other times, exciting or even relieving. Often the fear is actually about the letting go that precedes it. Once we do that, acceptance and transformation through changing circumstances in our lives can feel freeing and ultimately helpful and vitalising to our soul. There are many times when the prospect of changes within us, or in our circumstances, can fill us with a sense of fear as well as excitement. This oracle speaks to you now to allay any concerns. Your affairs are working out in accordance with a higher loving plan. No matter what your fears may be, changing circumstances will actually be much better for you.

150

No Need to Hide Yourself

Without realising it, sometimes we hold ourselves back, feeling like we must cultivate a certain appearance - physically, emotionally or otherwise - in order to be acceptable or make those around us happy. It is time for you to share more of your authentic being, not less. There is no need to fear judgement. Judgement hurts when we make it about ourselves and agree with the judgement. In such cases, there is an opportunity to heal the inner wound. When we do so, we recognise that judgement is not a truth, it is an expression of a wound in the person doing the judging. Have compassion for the mistakes that all of us make as humans. Choose to let go of shaming. Choose to feel good about who you are and recognise the eternally unstained innocence of your true inner being.

151

Embrace

When you are healing from toxic shame, there is an awakening of a new desire within the soul. That is the desire to share one's authentic self with others, so that one may truly be loved, and love, freely. This oracle brings encouragement to take a further step on your life path, perhaps branching out into new forms of self-expression, considering new connections or relationships, sharing yourself from a place of inner confidence and self-love, with nothing to hide. You are strong enough within yourself to reach out. Let your real self be seen and heard. Nurture the new and beautiful perceptions about yourself that are starting to break through negative self-talk. Grab on to the idea that you are beautiful, kind, capable of love, functional (if not a little crazy, in a good way), and marvellous. Nourish yourself with such food for the soul. As it strengthens you, your strength shall spontaneously flow to support others, too. Negativity is losing its battle with your soul. Make sure you lovingly and impressively finish it off.

152

Let it Live

After one has an intuition, a choice needs to be made to act upon it. This is when one often experiences the clash between soul and ego. As the soul wishes to move forward, the ego can create traps that undermine progress. One trap may be excessive fear based on feeling inadequate to the task, or an inflated and erroneous viewpoint that if something is destined, then no work is required on our part and it should effortlessly manifest, materialising out of thin air. It is good to have faith in the power of the Universe as our co-creative ally, although it does not do our tasks for us. Humans still need to hold up their side of things. Forgetting this can make the prospect of the hard work required to grow, be misinterpreted as a sign that something is not right, and therefore one should give up. You are meant to bring something to life. Do your work, but also allow the Universe to play a part in your manifestation. Seek a moderate approach for your best success. Do not talk yourself out of your destiny.

153

The Unexpected Path

The Universe has a degree of knowing that we, as humans, cannot possibly comprehend. Which means that at times, our life path is going to move in unexpected directions, as the greater guiding intelligence of the Universe unfolds, carrying all beings, including us, along for the ride. Although the unexpected twists in life may evoke curiosity, they might also evoke anxiety. When life isn't going in the direction that you want, take a moment to consider that the Universe loves you, is nurturing your spiritual fulfilment and you don't have to fight against life to have what will bring you peace and happiness. Let go of what you think you need and open up to the blessings that are being sent to you, now. There is something better on the horizon.

154

Assert the Soul

The heart holds a space for lovingly accepting all things, but wisdom provides the capacity to discern, to set boundaries and priorities, and to step away from mass ideals in order to distil one's own soul-oriented values and sense of meaning. Wisdom gives rise to authentic inner power that uplifts and transforms. This is in direct contrast to the mainstream definitions of power which tend to include the ability to put fear into others through judgement, that they may be controlled or dominated. Assert your soul values. Attend to what you know matters most. Do not be dissuaded by negative forces. Protect your mind, body and heart by immersing yourself in what is sacred to you. Continue to be the light that you are, bringing strength to others through how you choose to live and be in this world.

155

Evolving Vision

There is a time when certain visions or dreams - no matter how marvellous they are - need to be upgraded to meet with present circumstances. There is a spontaneous, wild and unpredictable quality to life that requires flexibility and responsiveness from those humans that wish to live creatively and connected to the endless emanations of divine play. Sometimes we have to grow to meet the vision. Sometimes the vision needs to grow to meet us! The Universe is lovingly prodding you to become aware that there is more depth and richness to your divine life path than you thought. Instead of a one-course meal, a sumptuous banquet is in order. It might seem counterintuitive, but it does take courage to receive. It does involve confronting our own previously unconscious smallness of mind or heart. Let smaller notions be stretched by the higher will of divine purpose. Be bold with your openness to what can be. Many new things are becoming possible for you now and through that, much benefit shall emerge for many.

156

Your World is Changing

Even if your conscious mind cannot yet recognise it, much is shifting in your inner world. There is an inner movement of psychic energies, gathering momentum, reverberating through your soul. As you are growing spiritually, you are naturally triggering purification of your soul and an old trauma is now ready to heal. When the inner self is healing, stored trauma can erupt for cathartic release through sudden emotional outbursts. There may not seem to be an external cause for the emotion. What is happening is healing, and therefore constructive. It can feel unsettling and even evoke judgement when one doesn't feel able to handle the emotions. Instead of judging, reach out for help. Recognise that you are courageous enough to be healing deep trauma. To reconnect to peace and a sense of solid spiritual ground after such releases, remind yourself that your body and soul know how to heal. There is something happening that is ultimately positive in long-term effect. You and your world are transforming in the best possible way.

157

Breaking Patterns

As you approach new ways of being, old identities often crack apart. This is because those identities were too limiting, like set roles you had to play, rather than flexible means by which you could express yourself. Those old roles kept real parts of your authentic self locked away. As you cast aside false and unduly limited views of yourself, the once-rejected or hidden parts can come out of hiding, and begin to heal, integrating with the rest of you. You are becoming more of the real you. Others may not always see it this way. Your change may trigger uncomfortable feelings for them (if they are not so willing to change and grow). Your change will inspire those who are ready to evolve. You don't need to be held in place by another's opinion of you. Embrace all parts of yourself so that you can settle peacefully into the knowledge of who you are and what you are here to do.

158

Dark Dealings

As your light becomes brighter in this world, you will perhaps attract the interest of wounded individuals that wish to tear you down, labouring under the misconception that somehow, that will make them more powerful. If you have become entangled in such a sorrowful state of affairs, then it is time to reinforce your connection to the beautiful light within you. There is always an opportunity for increasing self-liberation when caught up in negativity, gossip, slander or other mean-spirited behaviours. You have no need to defend yourself when you are at peace with who you are, and if after some reflection you feel the need to assert a simple truth calmly and openly, you can do so in a way that contributes positivity to an otherwise negative situation. You do not have to play by the rules set down by another. You don't have to play games with them.

159 A Positive Point of No Return

The more alive we are willing to become, the more we must be prepared to die a symbolic - and profound - psychological death, at certain times on our life journey. That symbolic death may be triggered by an ending, loss or disappointment, or the natural and gentle progress of life whereby certain phases of life end, allowing us to enter into a new role and way of being. If we can mourn these symbolic deaths, treating them with respect and acknowledgement, grieving in an authentic way, then they become sacrifices on the altar of new life. To ignore what is ending, for fear it means something terrible, denies us the chance to deeply participate and receive what is behind these endings (which is always a new beginning). You may be moving through loss or finding it difficult to let go of something that has been. Yet there is something truly beautiful and special that can emerge out of this process, if you allow it. There is more that is meant for you.

160

Initiation

Sometimes - though fortunately not always! - we gain what we need through a challenging experience. It can be a breaking open of what we once held sacred, so that we will not be confined by a life too small for our heart. Those moments are rarely easy, but it can help to remember that we are not being punished or harmed. There is nothing wrong, so much as the outgrowing of something in order to accommodate the growing capacity of the heart. Be present with what you are experiencing. Follow the journey from a perspective of inner healing rather than attempting to change outer circumstances by force. As you let go, you will see that the outer situation will naturally change once you are ready internally for it to do so. Working on the inner level will be what triggers outer change. Do not resist your own evolution. Trust where your path is leading you.

161

Guardians and Guides

No matter what your belief system may be, the heart has a capacity to attract the most loving, luminous, wise and helpful guardians and guides. Its sincere desire for help is enough to call in beneficial grace. Your belief system may prevent you from believing it is possible, or it may enhance your willingness to reach out. This oracle comes to you with a suggestion that you ask for help about whatever has been bothering you by calling upon those beings who love you unconditionally. There are wise ones who want to help you find an easier way to grow with grace rather than only through suffering. If you have already asked for help, consider this confirmation that you've been heard, and solutions are already manifesting. You may be wondering whether you can or should ask for spiritual help (and if this challenges your belief systems, you may also wonder if you are going nuts). This oracle says to ask anyway and know that being a little crazy is often a wise way to be.

162

Sense of the Subtle

Have you ever sensed something about a situation, only to talk yourself out of what you felt, and then later found out some piece of information that confirmed your initial intuition? The sense of the subtle can be startlingly accurate and helpful - and too easy to dismiss! This oracle brings you two messages. Firstly, there are signs of subtle but significant growth happening within your own soul. Continue to commit to your spiritual healing journey. In time, you will sense these changes within and in due course, they will bear luscious fruits of transformation on many levels. Secondly, tune in and pay heed to your spiritual insight. You are perceiving something that seems like a mere flicker but will in time burn bright with blazing clarity. Trust your intuition.

163

Align with Support

There are many encouragers, although sometimes we have to look a little deeper to find them, even reaching out beyond this physical realm into the spiritual worlds (where such support is enormous and incredibly enthusiastic). There are also those forces that have the intent to undermine and interfere with one's genuine spiritual progress. These trouble-making energies do not always appear to be negative on the surface. Sometimes they may appear to be positive, even though ultimately, they are distractions at best and therefore potentially damaging to our authentic soul journey. There is a strongly effective protective spiritual presence available to all who sincerely ask to be shielded from such negative agency. Such protection is not vengeful. It is enlightening. It doesn't create fear or separation - it keeps one connected to an ever-strengthening field of heart wisdom. You can call for such supreme spiritual protection with peace in your heart through your prayers and meditations. This protective divine hand is reaching for you now. All you need do is accept it wholeheartedly.

164

From Agony to Ecstasy

The path of becoming a fully embodied spiritual being is a process that often involves profound challenge through which we enter into our own suffering. With authentic presence to our experience, we grow in courage and eventually there is a spontaneous distillation of healing insight. It is a beautiful triumph, but it takes tremendous inner strength to stay the course. As we enter more deeply into our suffering - and reach beneath the symptoms into the source of the pain so that it can heal - we may wonder if it will ever end. This is especially true if you are breaking through a very old, entrenched pattern of suffering. It is important to remember that it will heal. You must continue to ask for spiritual assistance and remember that you are worthy of healing and that your pain is not a sign of wrongdoing on your part. Even if your suffering is, or has been great, this oracle predicts healing. You are enough of a divine badass to get through this.

165

Held by the Cosmic Madonna

When we suffer, our Universal Mother, the Cosmic Madonna, suffers along with us. She protects her children but never shields them from the mysteries of life, which - although painful at times - actually feed the soul with the richness of human experience. In your suffering, know that your divine mother has never turned away from you. Although she will always protect you from unnecessary struggle whenever you ask, certain experiences shall not be withheld from you if they are part of how you are becoming your full, marvellous self. Even so, you can feel her support and encouragement as you hold the tension of your struggles more lightly. You don't have to fixate or obsess about 'fixing' it. Though it may seem hard to understand logically, your struggle is blessed and will bring healing resolution that sets you free. In your own mind, imagine your struggles to be a sacred part of your soul empowerment. Pray not for the struggle to be taken away, but for the capacity to move through it. The blessing intended for you through this experience shall become one of your great heart treasures.

166

The Helpful Kind of Hope

True hopefulness – the sort that bestows the courage to continue with optimism and peace in our hearts – is not about closing our eyes and magically wishing our problems away. True hopefulness begins with acknowledging that something doesn't feel right and appears not to be working out. It takes hope to accept a change is needed, and to seek out resolution. Genuine, grounded optimism doesn't falsely say 'everything is fine', when it is not. Instead, it lets us know that when something isn't okay, there is a way to move forward so that things will be able to fall into place. When we acknowledge a pain, a problem or a situation, we conquer denial (and the undercurrent of anxiety it generates) and move into an open readiness to attract positive solutions. Speak openly about what you want to sort out. Trust that the Universe will respond constructively. There is a way through this.

167 What to do when you don't know what to do

If we are being honest with ourselves, a lot of the time we won't feel like we know what we are doing. That's not a bad sign, in fact it can be a good sign that we are daring to live outside our comfort zone of familiarity and certainty. The positive outcome of such a way of living is that we grow, often rapidly, and leave space for the Universe to work some healing magic in our lives. There can be some confusion however, about how to deal with complicated or unexpected situations. Often our intuition will spontaneously guide us but sometimes we'll feel that the answer to our troubles is frustratingly just beyond our reach. In such moments, we need help from the Universe to bridge the gap between our capacity and what is needed. If we trust the Universe, when the time is right, the next step becomes obvious. This is one of those times. You will know what you need to know, when you need to know it. Trust the Universe.

168 Explore Your Emotional Waters

It is time to let go of what you have been holding on to at an emotional level. Accessing emotions becomes easier with practice. It then allows you to tune into a different kind of knowing, an instinctive wisdom that keeps you connected to your immediate experiences. This is not about being right or blaming another. It's simply about owning your reality and being authentic. You do not need to make major decisions when in an emotional state, but once the waters have cleared and settled, you'll find decision making easier and will make wiser, less reactive choices. You have the capacity and the wisdom to take full responsibility for your life, and your healing journey becomes available to you as you do so. Spend some time in your inner world. Your feelings are leading you toward healing.

169 Starting Over

Your heart knows when it is time to leave something or someone behind as you move on with your life. All situations have a loving higher purpose to them, even the difficult ones that can evoke grief over loss. You don't need to force the pace of your own healing, but nor should you hide from your healing process through distractions or by keeping busy. You can only partake of the gift of starting over when you fully acknowledge what has run its course. It is time to put the past - especially a painful past - to rest. Whether that means simply letting go of the happenings of this particular day, or of a long-term commitment or condition. Only your heart can know in each moment. So, tune in and listen to what your heart is telling you. Starting over does not eradicate the valuable growth through your past experiences. It simply gives you a chance to begin with a fresh spiritual ledger, with many new possibilities and promises of grace. Be optimistic for what your life can be.

170

Growth Assured

When our dreams challenge what most people believe is possible, it is likely there will be occasional roadblocks and delays to deal with as our manifestation collides with some powerful opposing forces. The negative expectations of the world can cause even the brightest spirit to slump from time to time, losing energy and forgetting to trust in the Universe. This is when we need to remember our growth is assured. It is not a question of if, but rather of when, how and with whom. And those last three questions are mostly up to the Universe to decide. This oracle advises you to have patience and continue to commit to your work. Find the happy place where you are working toward your goal, unfazed by any perceived setbacks. Trust that what you are seeking actually wants to be created and so shall be.

171 Offering Troubles and Receiving Solutions

Handing over a problem to the Universe, and receiving the solution, can seem easy enough in theory. It is not until one tries to put this idea into practice that the difficulty becomes evident. We might believe we have handed something over, but if we are worrying about it five minutes later, or still have an underlying anxiety about it, then we have not accomplished the practice. Handing something over means completely surrendering any attachment to the outcome. You don't give up hope, but you do give up worry! Through genuine surrender, you feel relieved and experience the best results. You don't become passive, you become receptive. If you need to do something, you'll sense it. If you need to back off and let things unfold without your intervention, you'll sense that too. The Universe actually wants what is best for you. Don't get in its way.

172

Peace in the Process

When you are committed to becoming conscious, your life journey can feel like an endless series of growth-inducing opportunities, healing processes and adventures in consciousness-raising. In connection with the deeper place of stillness and peace beneath the ceaseless activity, we can find a happy balance between contentment and engagement. You can act, but from a more relaxed place. If you have found yourself caught up in stress, feeling overloaded, confused or unable to commit to what you most want to do, take a breath. Connect to your inner self. Come back to you, and what you are here to do (which is to be yourself). As you connect to your inner self, the outer will fall into place. There's no need to force the world to bend to your will. You'll find the outer way unfolds more effortlessly and graciously as you take your inner journey. Working on yourself will change your life in the most beautiful ways. Don't give up on yourself or the positive influence that your consciousness can generate for others.

173

Claim your Divine Dignity

Modern culture ignores the soul and derides the spirit with the belief that if one cannot perceive something with the five senses, then it is not real. Manipulation, comparison, judgement, belittlement and shaming pervade many human interactions. There are modern people who believe that you aren't in the 'real world' if you believe in spiritual matters. They ridicule those that do, judging them as naïve or delusional. Modern humanity is in desperate need of those individuals who genuinely aim to live from love, rather than from scarcity, power games and fear. To be such a wise soul in a collective that does not always have the capacity to recognise and value wisdom, is part of the spiritual test of being born a human in this era. Humans are designed to heal, to rise above such humiliations and disparagements. To do so requires seeing yourself clearly and hearing the truth beneath the lies you've heard. There is dignity, daring and sacred defiance within your heart. Let these become the fires of your own alchemical healing. Claim yourself.

174

Trust Your Spirit

We were born not to fear our bodies and deny our spirits, but to love the earth and fly with the wings of spiritual grace. Even with those invisible wings in our backs and the perfect current of sacred grace in the air, through which we can be raised into freedom and exhilaration, if we don't trust enough to leap, all this comes to nothing. Trusting the spirit is not some misplaced entitlement that the world owes us what our ego demands. Thankfully, the spirit is not governed by the immature tantrums of thwarted ego. Trusting spirit is about understanding that the spirit, in sacred connection with the earth, has the ability to manifest its light through a willing and capable human. It is a recognition that spirit wants what will truly bring you blissful fulfilment. Spirit is a very real part of you. You can rely upon its skilfulness, timing and resourcefulness. It knows what is needed, and when.

175

Rattling Cages Wide Open

The self-imposed prisons of the mind lock us into fearful doubt and confusion. The sacred feminine goddess wants us to be free. Through her encouragement, our inner goddess-loving rabble-rouser kicks open those cages and dares to step outside. There she is, standing in a field of wild flowers, hair blowing freely in the wind, calling to us. She says, "Come to me, beloved of mine, step into this life with me. We have much to share with each other and with the rest of the world. Let's go rattle some cages! Freedom is calling to all of my children!" Open your heart to her as you step free from your own controlling nature. Life wants to bring a new freedom and liberation into your heart, mind and life. It may not always feel safe and yet you can trust it implicitly. This oracle indicates a significant spiritual breakthrough is at hand.

176

Cardiognosis

The heart has its own knowing. Cardiognosis, or heart-knowing, isn't interested in wrong and right, judgement or one belief system over another. The soul wants to thrive, and in that, have all beings thriving, because it understands unity and interdependence as a reality rather than a concept. It knows that no matter how impressive or spiritual an argument may sound, if the intention or effect behind a communication is divisive, based in fear, dominance or control, then it is not of love and is therefore false. When we are in tune with the soul, our way becomes clearer. We discern more readily, without judgement, with wisdom. We don't need to overthink because we are clear in what we intuitively recognise. There is something that your heart, just knows. There is no need to engage in complicated arguments. Be guided by your heart.

177

Hungry for Life

Underneath all hunger - whether it seems to be for material possessions or particular substances - lies a deep soul hunger for life. It can only be sated through the soul, through the capacity to directly experience life in all of its mystery. The mind cannot accomplish this. It has no feeling function. The body alone cannot do it. It has no self-awareness. It is the mind and body united, through the soul, which creates the capacity for experience that is alchemical, healing and nourishing. Without soul, it is like being at the banquet, with no mouth to eat. Surely this is a definition of hell. Your hungers will be met. Allow yourself to acknowledge what it is that you yearn for and know that life shall generously provide. Give yourself permission to eat. Connect your mind and body lovingly, and your soul can grow to feast upon the banquet of experience that life provides. There is a legitimate hunger within you and life is more than willing to provide what is needed to fulfil you.

178

Divine Direction

The quickest path to a destination is not often the most obvious or direct route. There can be pitfalls on the logical path only evident to the all-seeing divine eye. In compassion, the Universe will nudge you along a better path. To the more limited human perspective, the path may not seem better at all. It may seem longer, yet without the problems that you are yet to encounter on the more obvious path, it will end up being a more graceful and swift approach. When a door is closed to you, there is no need to turn away. It is better instead to affirm that the Universe is up to something (good) and become open to another way. It may or may not materialise immediately. Remember that divine timing is always at play. This oracle informs you that divine direction (or perhaps redirection) is happening in your life. Be curious and open to what is, not remaining attached to plans, but being willing to adapt according to the circumstances. Believe that the Universe is always working with you to manifest your brightest and most beautiful sacred fulfilment.

179

The Moon at Her Feet

When we are sinking under the weight of negative thinking and emotional suffering, her spiritual strength is there to lift us. When we are struggling to sustain new patterns of healing change, her grace is there to protect us from falling back into old psychological patterns. Her power overcomes the gravity of habit that we are - as yet - unable to vanquish on our own. She is our helping hand so that we can successfully attain the strength needed to seed new ways of being, helping them develop until we are strong enough to carry them forward ourselves. This oracle speaks of important attempts to outgrow old patterns and of divine intervention to assist with this process. Lean into the grace of the goddess and be supported in all of your efforts. Success will come.

180

The Transcendent Choice

In the experience of conflict, two viewpoints are in opposition. Conflict can be an important trigger for our personal growth, like the friction that creates sparks and fuels the fires of transformation. However, if the conflict has become wearying, and constructive energy is no longer derived from the tension, then it is time for the third way - the transcendent choice that elevates one's consciousness from opposition and disharmony into higher functioning and integrated being. In opening one's heart to an inner experience of spiritual connection, the new vision, psychological reframe and emotional relief, shall emerge. There is an answer that shall bring relief. Forget about who is right and who is wrong. Be willing to give up the fight and you'll see the light.

181 Abundance Blessing

When we are focused on fear for our survival, we can become temporarily blinded to the reality of what we possess internally and the willingness and capacity that the Universe has for providing us with more. If it seems that part of our life is in decline, it is simply because the energy of abundance is flowing into another area so that it may prosper. In due course, the flow shall return to rectify whatever matter has been of concern. There is no need to fixate or become afraid. Fears are often a habitual reaction to a distorted perception rather than an accurate reflection of what is taking place. Be kind to the fearful parts of you. Allow them to heal as you open up to the Universe, calling upon its generosity and grace to support the healing. There is so much waiting for you. Do not close yourself down. Open your heart and let it in.

182

Real Love

Even deeply inspired hearts will sometimes waiver, feel tired or tested in faith or wonder if the path is true and if the heart's genuine need for authentic connection in a real, nourishing and palpable way can ever be fulfilled. This oracle brings a message for those who have been subject to doubts or delays, finding it difficult to know whether a situation will work out in a satisfactory way. You have the real love of the Universe within you. Don't allow anything or anyone to subdue your spirit. Dare to believe that you can give up your doubts and that you don't need to be afraid. The love within you has remarkable wisdom and healing power. There are those that want and need that love, including you. Sometimes we just need a gentle reminder to drop everything else and come back to the heart with trust.

183

Deepening

On the spiritual path, there is always somewhere further to travel, a deeper experience to be had, more love to be. Sometimes we are working so hard on outer world matters that we forget there is a beautiful inner journey happening for us and that tuning into it, is like dipping into a restorative well. This oracle brings the message of a new level of spiritual experience opening up to you. To cross the threshold into that vaster inner ocean of beauty, grace and higher consciousness, there may be a purification process required. Such a process will prepare your mind and body to be able to handle the increased power of a pure love and spiritual light. Purification can arise in any area of your life, bringing up issues so that you can attain clarity and inner healing. If you are confronted with any issue, know that this is a sign of progress. What is being brought to your attention is done so to free you from constriction and deception. Whether you can make sense of what is happening, your heart and soul will be fed by it. This oracle brings good tidings.

184

Pause to Progress

There is a time for work and a time for rest. Without these in balance, creation cannot happen. There is a tendency to misunderstand and dismiss the need for rest. True rest gives us a chance for replenishment, to stop thinking about our problems and in that spaciousness, allow for a refreshed and more constructive viewpoint to emerge. In rest, we are given a chance to settle deep into our being. We become receptive to spiritual connection. Whilst this oracle does not advise abandoning a path or purpose, it does suggest that this is not a time to keep forging ahead. Take a pause. Recalibrate and replenish. When it is time to resume activity, your continued progress is assured.

185

Wisdom of Winter

The genius and mystery of the spiritual realm is that its truth is often the exact opposite of what human perspective assumes. When nothing appears to be happening, it can be that everything is in a critical point of flux at a deeper level. This is why we attend to our spiritual practices - such as prayer, journaling, contemplation and meditation, or whatever forms of healing purification we feel guided to do - and then trust in the outcome unconditionally. Even in the absence of immediate results! This oracle brings notice that even in the stillness of winter, when the earth is resting, there is much preparation taking place to ensure the flowering and buzz of activity as new life emerges in the spring. Do not lose hope. There is more happening than you realise, even if you cannot see it yet. Have patience and know that your time shall come.

186

Strengthen Your Sanctuary

The pure hearted need a sanctuary to which they can regularly seek graceful shelter from the violence and ills of the world. It may be symbolic, a place within your heart where you rest in meditation at the beginning and end of each day. It may also be a physical space in which you practice your symbolic return to sanctuary. You do not need to dismiss the troubles you are seeking to resolve in your life and in our world. Nor do you need to be tortured by them. In your inner sanctuary, you can find peace and respite. Ask for graceful intervention on behalf of all in need, and then let it go as you rest in sacred connection with love. Stay in the power of your heart. Let it surround and comfort you. You do not need to attempt to force anything. Love is practical and knows the way. Do not underestimate what love can accomplish.

187 Comfort for When You are in Pain

When you or a loved one are in pain, or your heart is troubled by the pain that you see in the world, it is time to reach for spiritual comfort - for yourself and for all beings caught in suffering. There is an expansive channel of grace that is able to bring relief, soothing higher perspective, and gentle presence to calm and alleviate emotional distress. This spiritual channel can operate through many willing vessels, connecting with those beings that suffer, bringing relief. Your caring heart is your authority to call upon this channel of love, grace and healing now and at any time you feel it is needed. There is no limit on your permission to call upon it, no limit on how much that spiritual wisdom wants to help and can assist all beings in need. Call upon it with faith in your heart. Let the experience be so real to you that you know you are activating and participating in a living field of kindness that touches and heals.

188 Healing from Disappointment and Loss

The suffering of loss or disappointment has unfolded in your life as a sacrifice of what could have been, on the altar of a different future. Grieve what has not come to pass, and what has been lost. Grieve because the love in your heart felt the preciousness and hopefulness of what once was or could have been. Let your heart be cleansed through the grieving, which is also a powerful way of honouring, of having gratitude and saying, "Thank you for the valuable power this has held for my soul". Then the grace of letting go will happen naturally with your readiness, not from force or misused willpower. What has happened in the past can either imprison you or free you. Your heart is capable of the latter. Let it lead the way. In time, you shall naturally and joyfully attune yourself to that which shall emerge out of the spaciousness created by this letting go.

189

Strength of the Gentle

The strongest are called upon to aid those in need. The Universal heart empowers such sacred purpose and acts through willing channels, protecting and guiding those that serve a greater guiding hand. Your light can be of assistance without you realising it. Your presence in a toxic environment or situation might be what is preventing further decay or even helping to turn it around. One cannot often know the mysterious workings of a greater spiritual plan, yet one can trust in its wisdom. Through your inner spiritual connection, you can come back into balance, resting upon stable inner spiritual ground, even if the world around you appears to be spinning out of control. Calling upon divine love with a sincere heart, asking for protection and assistance, is enough. You are being utilised as an instrument of higher workings. Align and surrender to the best of your ability and trust in the protective nature of its grace.

190

Meant for You

There is something beautiful -perhaps yet unseen - on your horizon that is meant for you. What your soul wants and needs has been summoned by the spiritual power of your heart. Opportunity is the Universe believing in you. Return the compliment by accepting what enters your world with open arms and a trusting heart. All paths lead us to where we need to be, so even if this one involves the unexpected, you can be sure that you are heading in the right direction. Play with the thought that you deserve goodness and don't be shy to receive it. Drop the fear and open yourself to what is meant to be.

191

Better than Expected

Whatever has been troubling you is going to work out better than expected. You won't necessarily see it coming, but relief and reinvention are imminent. It is not a question of whether or not resolution shall come - it will do so - but a question of timing. Trust that all matters in your life are going to work out. Not only that, but also the matter that seems to be the darkest or most troubling, is going to be what brings forth the most beautiful healing gift. Allow the Universe to show you its generous and good intentions, as what once appeared to be a problem dissolves and reforms itself into positivity and light. Hold on to your optimism.

192

Stunning Rebirth

Even the most apparently inevitable ending is not really the end. There is a chance for complete release that unleashes energy to be reborn in a new form. You can think that something is over, that the eleventh hour is upon you, that the opening chords of your swan song is sounding ... and you may have given up. But then, out of the ashes like some stunning and startling phoenix, there is a resurrection. Everything changes. Just like that. From freefalling to soaring in an instant. Fate steps in, destinies are restored, and life demonstrates its creative potency. Give up your hold on things, but do not give up your hope. Allow things to fall away. Trust that life knows how to bring the right elements together at the right time and will do so, irrespective of whether it seems possible at the moment. There is a demonstration of the (apparently) impossible made possible in your future.

193

Tiger Angel

There will be moments when we wonder whether we are doing a great job at living this life of ours. We may want to contribute to the collective but question whether it is even possible when our own struggles demand so much time and energy. Remember that the desires in your heart have been placed there for higher purpose. The heart yearns for fulfilment, and what will best bring fulfilment differs for each individual, based on capacity. The fulfilment of one heart contributes to the fulfilment of all hearts, because the heart is connected consciousness. Trust in what you yearn for. Know that it is not selfish to pursue it, for the benefit of manifestation shall reach farther than you can consciously recognise. You have the light of an angel and the fierceness of a tiger in your heart. You are capable of more than you realise.

194

Hold to Your Truth

In our wise intention to remain open minded, we can run the risk of being bombarded with differing opinions, ideas and conflicting information. To remain aware of your own inner truth during such information overload requires some strength of mind. You can be interested and curious in the viewpoints of others, whilst filtering all through your own internal process of discernment. This oracle cautions against allowing yourself to be swayed by another, no matter how impressive their argument may seem. That which is original, different and of a higher perspective is not always immediately understood or received. Yet it is so needed in our world. So, stay true to what you see and know, gentle but unwavering. Consider other views, but let your inner knowing be your ultimate guide.

195

Big Picture Success

The pleasure of gratification is sometimes better delayed - for more pleasure and greater success, later! There is a grander scheme unfolding, which will ultimately be of benefit to you. Any delay, obstacle, loss or perceived failure at this time is a twist in the plot of your life, necessary for the gracious plan to unfold. Remember that fear and doubt are little more than symptoms of fatigue. Your soul needs some replenishment, some playfulness and time out, to restore its optimism, determination and joie de vivre. This oracle encourages you stay confident, and to give yourself some time off for renewal. You may have heard the expression that sometimes we need to lose the battle to win the war. Know that any short-term losses are not going to steal away your long-term victory.

196 Cutting the Cords of Connection

Unlike the loving spiritual bonds that connect us all, heart to heart, psychic cords can link us to memories, fears and people that we would rather not be connected to because they are not healthy for us. Cutting the cords allows your energy to be with you, rather than leaking away. Clearing such cords will re-establish an appropriate psychic boundary that keeps you open to receive from life whilst containing what is rightfully yours (such as your energy). The way to cut cords, is to make the decision to do so. Realise that you don't have to energetically finance the negativity of others. You can do more for all beings - including yourself - by being the strongest light you can be right now.

197

Vision of the Priestess

The priestess is one who lives in the physical world with strong spiritual sight that enables access to signs and information from the realms of guardians and guides. Such otherworldly priestess wisdom is available to us through her temple, which is the heart. To access such helpful secret knowledge, one must be willing to let go of belief in appearances. Belief in appearances keeps the door to the temple closed. As the expression goes - appearances can deceive. There is more to a particular situation in your life than meets the eye. Look beneath what appears to be and trust in what you sense in your most relaxed, open and curious moments, centred peacefully in your heart. One cannot force a vision, but one can be open to its arrival as a welcome guest in the sacred space of the heart. It will bring glad tidings and wisdom to successfully navigate the troublesome complications that can arise in our own minds. You'll see what you need to see and find relief through that vision.

198

From Distraction to Focus

The creative spirit within has rightfully been throwing something of a temper tantrum. It wants to create and the constant distractions that you are allowing to steal your time and attention are getting in the way. Summon your determination to conquer procrastination, and put other priorities to one side, even if just for a time. You must allow the inner creation the time and attention it needs to take shape. This is not a flight of fancy but a deep inner need. In meeting the needs of the soul, you are moving forward on your life path in such a way that the Universe is empowered to assist you. Get focused on what matters to you. Don't squander your precious energy on worrying about things you cannot change. Attend to your work, and then all else can, and will, fall into place.

199

Go to Ground

There are rare moments where rather than steady, quiet inner growth, there is a shift that manifests like a wild explosion of pent-up inner energies. There are times when such extroverted energies are needed to push through barriers and propel the soul to the next level of freedom to create, be and commit to one's sacred tasks, free from interference. Such short duration, high-intensity explosive awareness can send shock waves rippling through one's being and life. It can take some time to methodically and gently integrate what has been stirred up as a result of the sacred disturbance. One can feel unstable and feel the need to go to ground, taking some time out to make sense of things. Make sure you do this through whatever rocks your world - whether it seems to be good or bad, there is a greater healing purpose at work. To honour this, dispense with the need to return to what was and explore the ways that you can ground, settle and live in the here and now.

200

Shedding

This oracle brings a loving reminder that you don't need to hold on to a support system, belief or connection, out of fear. Sometimes it's just time to let it go. If you try to hold on, you will actually be holding yourself back. Maybe you can reconnect from a different perspective later on, or perhaps it really is a complete letting go at this time. You don't have to know now. You just need to steady yourself and focus on what is happening in the depths of your being. Whatever is meant to be part of your future cannot be lost to you through such a process. The heart knows how to let go and how to attract. It may feel like you are going crazy, but you aren't. In letting go, you are entering sacred territory where the past cannot enter. Through such daring, you will glimpse the new world opening up for you.

201

Flying Fish

Abilities, gifts, new ways of seeing and being are rising up from the depths of your soul. Within the hidden depths, rests undiscovered magic and its time has come. It wants to be caught, leaping up from your oceanic consciousness, like a flying fish. There needs to be space set aside for such sacred emergence. One cannot birth new realities when entirely consumed in what already exists. There must be some energy to spare for sacred conception. Gather your psychological and emotional strength to set aside some time and space for inner contemplation. Imagine that what is being cultivated on an inner level shall become the apple of your eye and cherished above all else. Give that which the heart recognises as being worthwhile its due.

202 The Bright Side

As helpful as experiences of darkness can be on the spiritual path, when you feel like you've had more than enough of it to last a lifetime, then you know it's your time to step into the light. It takes courage to enter the darkness of life's mysteries, and courage to step out of darkness into the light. To do so requires letting go of your attachment to drama, to the stories, suffering and pain of the past. You don't need to deny a painful past, but you can recognise that it is possible to open your heart to trust, love, reassurance, commitment and comfort again. Set aside your mental anguish by affirming that on this day, you choose to trust that the Universe loves you and is unfolding a plan that has your best interests at heart. Believe wholeheartedly that life is working for you, not against you. Step into the light.

203 Unconditional Generosity of Your Light

To choose to shine your light, regardless of whether others around you understand, acknowledge or recognise it, speaks of an unconditional generosity of spirit. It also indicates wisdom. The sun shines whether we hide under a shady tree or lie scantily clad beneath its rays. Either way it provides light and encourages life to flourish on this earth. Imagine the negative repercussions if it decided not to shine. Those beings who need the direct experience of your light will find their way to you, and you can rest in the knowledge that even those seemingly resistant to it, gain benefit. Your generosity attracts the generosity of the Universe to you. Stand wherever you are, and shine with trust, patience and courage. There is much that the Universe seeks to bring into the world through your faithful heart.

204

Sunshine Soul Cleanse

A beautiful and simple statement for cleansing the soul using your freewill and the power of your voice: "I call on the light and sound of unconditional love. You fill me and surround me with your protective emanation of healing, grace, mercy, compassion and wisdom. Anything not of unconditional love now leaves my mind, body and soul. I choose to place my trust, and my being, in the light." To step it up a notch, you can pretend you are the most enthusiastic, divine cheerleader for the light that ever was. You can shake your soul pompoms and cheer for a victorious, golden shining sun above your head by saying, "Ra! Ra! Ra!"

205

Quiet Wisdom

There is wisdom in knowing when to speak and when to remain quiet. The value of the personal can be dismissed too readily, as though something doesn't really matter unless it is seen publicly. When it is time to share with others, you'll recognise it and sense that it is coming from a place of honouring and respect for what is offered, rather than seeking external validation to prop up a lack of inner valuing. Keeping certain things out of the public eye until the right time - or perhaps always - is also a method of protection from those who do not have healthy boundaries and, through jealousy or other wounded behaviour based on ill will, are intent on disparagement or destruction. Keep your treasures to yourself until you sense the capacity to stand true in your essence, regardless of the play of darkness and light around you.

206 New Worlds are Calling You Forth

When our world has become too small for our spirit, it can feel painful, like trying to walk in shoes that we've outgrown. Doing it for too long can leave one feeling crippled with pain and unable to walk. Your spirit is yearning to encounter new worlds of experience. The Universe is responding to that need by broadening your horizons. You may welcome the unfamiliar, even when it seems intimidating or unappealing. Know that you shall find a way to flourish. You always do! You may reside in these new worlds or choose to pass through on your way to yet more adventure. You are destined to embark upon new adventures and something of value is awaiting you. Let your spirit kick off your shoes, run barefoot and free along the beautiful path unfolding before you now.

207

Secret Knowledge Unveiled

More often than not, there is further information that - as it comes to light - shall help one formulate a more accurate assessment of a situation. This oracle brings a message that there is information you are yet to discover. You don't need to be concerned, but you do need to take care not to force a decision based on incomplete or even potentially misleading information. You cannot know what you do not know - so it is sensible to wait until a clearer vision becomes available to you. If what you see, sense or think is negative, remember that you are yet to glean the whole picture. Be patient and open to further insight. A revelation, and a helpful shift in perspective, is on its way.

208

Future Bright and Blessed

The mind tends to look back at what has been and make assumptions about what shall continue to be in the future. Yet such an approach discounts the possibility of something bright and new entering your world, something that positively expresses the effects of your courageous inner work and the creative bent of the spirit. You shall leave the storms of the past behind. Your feet are destined to settle upon sacred ground, where calm shall prevail inside and out. Don't lose hope for what can be. You are capable of gaining wisdom from your experiences without turning them into predictions for your future. Deal with what you must and then put the past to rest. It is time to start afresh and believe in the positive power of this moment and your future.

209 Authentic Eccentric

This oracle speaks of being your own person, an offbeat individual refusing to fall into the plans that others make for you. In a world where we are taught that we need permission to do almost anything, it takes guts to decide to give yourself unconditional permission to be unconditionally yourself. Permission to accept your strangely beautiful, weirdly wonderful and divinely eccentric authenticity, generates a charisma that attracts inspirational energy and creative pathways. Many fear this kind of individuality. They don't understand that it is not about selfishness but about being able to give radically and freely. You can have compassion for such fear whilst not buying into it. Allow yourself to shake things up a little. When it's about your inner journey and done from a place of love - not about arrogantly assuming you have the right to impose yourself upon another - it will open up inspired pathways.

210

Fight Without Fighting

Darkness can consume the light of hope, but it can also be made to serve the light through spiritual skilfulness that utilises one's experience of darkness, to grow positive traits within the soul. To do this, you have to know how to fight without fighting. Forget about the rules of war established by fear-enslaved minds. Create your own rules, not based on what others want you to believe, but based on what works to keep your heart liberated. There is no need to try to convince anyone of anything nor force a resolution. The stronger you are, the more you will set up resistance if you approach matters directly. You want your power to work for you, not against you. What would resolution feel like? Focus on the feeling, the joy and light of it. Grow it in your heart. Relax and trust that genuine, heartfelt affirmation is a brilliant countermove, lifting you out of the war zone and into the truth of your spirit.

211 A Loving Invitation to Universal Wisdom

There are some things, which human intelligence cannot manage to resolve, and an invitation to universal wisdom is going to be the best course of action to obtain the most desirable outcome for all. Here is a simple statement for you to invoke such wisdom for any matter of concern. "I call on the unconditional love of the Universe as my guide, protector, friend and witness. I now release anything or anyone attempting to influence me away from unconditional love and trust in the highest wisdom. I call into my body, mind and heart the presence of true wisdom. I choose to give up the drama and the judgement and, to the best of my ability, become a channel for compassion and wisdom. May spiritual grace more than compensate when my capacity or action falls short of what can best serve the spiritual benefit of all beings."

212

Real Allies

It is time to attract the real allies of your heart. Those who are not interested in what you can do for them, but who love you for who you really are. You are ready to opt out of a game that most people play unconsciously. It's a game of image at the expense of the true self. Yet any promise of love or success that begins with you contorting yourself into something you are not, is a false promise. It cannot deliver anything worthy of you. All it does is starve the authentic self behind masks of limited self-definition and identity. You are destined for a more real, true and wild experience of love. Open to it within yourself first, and then you can share it with others, successfully discerning the glitter from the gold. Remember that sometimes you have to say 'no' in order to say 'yes'. Seek the company of those with whom you share a real heart-connection, be they in the world or in the realm of spirit.

213

Outsmarting Wickedness

You are meant to be a sun, shining bright even in the dark cold depths of winter. There are some who don't like the light. They will sense any wavering in your feeling of self-worth and set out to exploit, enhance and increase it. Don't let them! Shine your light with sacred stubbornness and divine defiance. Remember that those who try to freeze one's heart with cold glances of criticism, judgement or ridicule do not hold power over your soul. They will want you to believe that they do. Yet your soulful passion has more than enough fire to melt such icy invaders and preserve the love that rightfully warms your world.

214 Sweetheart

There is much violence in our world, in our minds, in our attitudes toward ourselves and others. Many assume that this is acceptable because it is so common. They forget that they have a right to question and change it. Even the most ambitious aims for the healing transformation of our human collective, begins with us as individuals. Regret, shame, judgement, fear of not being good enough and the constant push to become more, are all forms of violence. These behaviours and beliefs create invisible bruises that cannot heal unless we give ourselves the sweetness, kindness and compassion we need to break free from the abusive cycle. This oracle indicates a gentler and kinder way of being is on offer to you. Will you claim it for yourself and others?

215 Honour Your Inner Process

Hold your feelings and insights in high enough regard that you take the time necessary to consider them. If you do not give yourself enough space to distil your own thoughts and feelings on certain matters, you cannot know how it is best to proceed, or indeed, if any action needs to be taken at all. Rather than acting immediately from an emotional state, pause, contemplate, and give things time to settle so that if you do act, it is with clarity and peacefulness. You will not unnecessarily be fuelling fires, nor will you be avoiding conscious action. You have wisdom within you. Take some time to tune into it with grace, patience and curiosity.

216 Dare to Leave, Dare to Return

There is a unique wisdom gained through the perspective of the outsider. You gain an ability to know who you are, without social pressures to conform, and you have the opportunity to develop different viewpoints and ways of understanding human beings and the world in which we dwell. One can become used to standing apart from the crowd, functioning as something of a lone wolf. But that is meant to be an experience, not an identity. There comes a time when you will give and gain most by reconnecting to and sharing your treasures with the community in ways, that feel most authentic and empowering for you and your tribe. You have daring within you. Use it!

217

Sovereignty of Self

To be in possession of one's self requires the acceptance and claiming of all of one's being. We come to this point through a journey of inner healing. This can be difficult but those who claw their way from shame, judgement and violation, into a full and loving possession of the self, cultivate an impressive inner strength through the process. The resulting self-acceptance makes these souls immune to being tricked or seduced into handing their power over to others, as though the approval of another means more than one's own self-love and self-respect. You can be amongst the crowd, feel at home in this world, love and be loved, and know the peace and acceptance that comes with belonging entirely to yourself.

218

Divine Disguise

Some blessings are well and truly hidden, disguised as a healing crisis or challenge. The mask can be so convincing that we are in no mood to deal with it, and want it gone from our lives immediately! You have every right to set boundaries regarding what you accept and do not. However, before you banish the offensive situation from your realm, consider that it may be an invitation to inner healing. It is not about excusing unacceptable behaviour, nor about denying your own right to choose what path you take. Sometimes you will be able to engage in darker experiences with full possession of your light secured, and at other times, it will be wiser and more lovingly protective of your light to simply walk away. In this instance, find a happy medium. Investigate a little, distil hidden helpfulness for your personal growth, and then set a strong boundary. Do trust that something good can come from all of this.

219

Obstacles of Grace

What would you think if you arrived at your destination ahead of schedule only to find that the town you were meant to visit hadn't even been founded yet? You may conclude that you must have got it wrong and go looking for another town to visit or completely invalidate your own intuition and take up another course of action. An over-enthusiastic approach, and too few obstacles, could lead to failure even though success seemed predictable. To save you from such a disastrous confusion and undermining of your sacred life task, the Universe is kindly slowing you down with a few strategically placed obstacles here and there. These obstacles come with the added benefit of developing your strength and determination, making your arrival in the town all the more impressive - and timely.

220 Narrow Your Choices Down to One

For many people, one of the gifts and challenges of modern life is the abundance of choice. It can create a crippling sense of anxiety and fuel procrastination. Yet, we only need to be denied our choices for a short time to realise that it is a freedom worth having. Abundance of choice can teach us how to radically improve our capacity for simplicity, discernment, patience and the art of overcoming distractions. Now that's an amazing spiritual skill set to develop and one that will serve you and the community in so many ways. For now, this oracle advises that you make one choice and to get to work on it. If you try to do everything right now, your productivity won't increase anywhere near as much as your stress level. Don't let the fear of missing out cause you to miss out on everything. Choose a path and go for it. The fulfilment of each individual step shall manifest the greater fulfilment of your path and potential.

221

Big Vision, Small Steps

This oracle brings encouragement for your grander and bolder visions. No matter how small and practical, or vast and impossible your vision may seem (from your current point of view), the step to your success is always the same. It is simply to take the next step available to you. No matter whether that is attending to a mundane task or taking a spiritual leap of faith, take that step. Then the next step becomes available to you. And so, the journey to manifestation unfolds. Though there may be so much to do, you can accomplish truly magnificent feats if you are willing to take one step at a time. Believe that your visions are attainable.

222 Velvet Queen

This oracle speaks of a shift from a belief of scarcity to one of prosperity where one can receive precious gifts with an open attitude of ease, neither holding on to them out of fear nor pushing them away out of shame or guilt. The significance of the Velvet Queen is that she heralds an inflow of abundance into your life. She also indicates that a rare accomplishment is within reach, through a combination of your own efforts and spiritual grace. You cannot make the sweetest fruit at the top of the tree grow any faster. That is in the realm of the rhythm of life. However, you can certainly do your part to foster its growth and your own strength, so that you are ready to climb the tree at the opportune moment. And when you're given a helping hand to navigate the trickier moments of your ascent, you can choose to accept it. Your success can benefit many. Embrace it.

223 Savouring

To acknowledge how far you have come can be useful. It evokes gratitude and renews commitment. Without those moments of appreciation and acknowledgement, one might feel lost in the journey, wondering if the Promised Land will ever appear, or question whether it even exists. Sometimes it is beneficial to lift one's attention from the daily tasks to gain some perspective. There would have once been a time when you dearly wished for all you have now, and likely a time in future when you shall have attained what it is that you currently seek. Savour your accomplishments, so far. Recognise what you have done and soak it in. Gain strength and peace from it. Affirm yourself, and you'll gain not only the renewed commitment to continue but also the joyful anticipation of further fulfilment.

224

One Last Drop

Like a vast container of water almost at its threshold, there may only be one more drop required to reach fulfilment. That last drop makes all the difference. Apparently and suddenly, all of what has been in development overflows and an astonishing abundance flows. Prior to that shift, there was likely no sense of how close such a turning point was. The modern world tends to focus on the turning point as if it could happen in isolation, forgetting the reality of all the preparation, effort and sacrifice - physical and spiritual - required to stay true to one's course, so that this offering may reach completion. This oracle encourages your continued application to your tasks and brings notice of imminent success.

225 Growing into Not Knowing

You have come to a place in your life where you don't know what's happening. You don't know who you are (well, not all of who you are). You don't know what you don't know. You are at the point of not knowing because you are growing. The more certain one is about life, the more likely one has been hanging around a particular fishbowl of belief systems for far too long. You've been brave enough to venture into wilder unchartered waters. It is not a bad sign that you wonder what you're doing and where you are going. Leaving known worlds does not mean that you are deviating from your path. It means that you are willing to experience more of what life has to offer and translate those experiences into wisdom. This wisdom is not always easily won, but it shall most certainly be of considerable value. You don't have to understand something to gain benefit from it. It's okay not to have all the answers right now.

226

Uncommon Sense

There's much to be said for common sense, practicality and a grounded approach, especially in regard to one's spiritual journey. However, to live creatively from a place of inner inspiration and spiritual guidance, one also needs to learn how to lean into the uncommon sense. Following a true vision of the soul inevitably leads us into uncomfortable and challenging spaces. The rapturous joy that fulfilment brings is not accessed without first jumping through a number of initiatory hoops. Such tests develop the capacity for uncommon sense, to live an ordinary and extraordinary life according to inner truth rather than imposed outer values. Listen to your common sense and your uncommon sense. Rather than opposing each other, they complement each other exceptionally well. There is a way to move through this situation that makes sense to your soul even though an army of others may tell you that you are mad. Don't be afraid to trust in what truly resonates for you.

227

The Joker is Wild

There's nothing impossible - or predictable - when the cosmic trickster appears. The Joker is the highest trump, the card to beat all others. Her presence here indicates that you are empowered to overcome all odds stacked against you. Whether it seems another may have the upper hand, or you feel like lone prey about to mauled by a pack of hungry predators, the Joker always wins. She comes out unexpectedly and changes destinies like a turning of the Wheel of Fortune. However, the Joker is also wild. Whilst you may be happy to see her in principle, in effect, you cannot know how she will accomplish her loving tricks. You are unlikely to see it coming and it may well subvert much of what you once held to be true. Even if she startles you like a sudden bright light in the middle of the night, you will benefit from her antics.

228

Thousand Arms of the Goddess

In numerous spiritual traditions, various depictions of divine beings feature them with more than two arms. One can interpret this to mean that the divine consciousness - in the Universe, and in us - is not limited to what a human can ordinarily accomplish. You are capable of many things and the fulfilment of your soul purpose will ask much of you. There will be many inspirations that you yearn to bring to life. This oracle speaks of the ultimate divine multi-tasker bringing much welcomed guidance. Come back to the present moment. Prioritise. Do what can be done now. Be open to genuine help and say no to the pseudo-helpers that make things more complicated than they need to be. This oracle speaks of great accomplishments in this world, for a collective benefit. The hands of the Divine Mother can give, and also take away. You can trust, however, that her hand is a genuinely helpful one.

229 Butterfly to Be

The butterfly has been imbued with an innate capacity for radical transformation. So too do you have natural instincts within, guiding you to grow in dramatic, utterly life-changing ways. The radical changes of which you dream, are meant to be. Trust in what is happening. Don't limit yourself unnecessarily for you are capable of beautiful, unlikely creations. This oracle brings prophecy of new life. Progress is your perfection. Growth is your sacred attainment. There is no need to shun what you have been. Wear your growth as a sacred crown of power. You could not be where you are now, or where you will be, without having had the experiences you had. Accept, release and allow what is destined to be.

230 She Who Stands at the Crossroads

This oracle heightens awareness that it is time for a new phase of life to begin. You cannot continue without making a choice, a commitment to what matters to you, a decision to see something through or to let it go. Patiently feel for the truth of your choice. Do not feel the need to make decisions that you will be forced to cling to for the rest of your life! This is one choice point, one crossroad. There will be others that arise along your path. However, you cannot continue to take every element of your life, your way of thinking and being, through the crossing into the next phase. Give yourself permission to take with you only what feels necessary to your heart. Give all else over to life to do what best serves all beings.

231

Inelegant and Worthy

At times, we feel like we have lost our footing and are clumsily stumbling about, making mistakes and a mess of things, even if our intentions are good. This can make us second-guess our choices and path in life. Whilst it's good to learn from things that didn't work out, shaming oneself and feeling bad about your journey can prevent you from making choices that tend to flow better when you are feeling good about yourself. This oracle recommends that you eschew shaming, ridiculing or guilt-inducing behaviour from within or around you. You have enough connection with yourself to be able to learn from your mistakes (which is why they are more accurately referred to as 'learning opportunities'). Be inelegant when you stumble, for your innate value is not compromised by your humanity.

232 Chin Up, Eyes Straight Ahead

In a disturbingly common and savage (il)logic, some like to tear others down to make themselves feel better about who they are. You are strong enough to overcome such lazy mean-spirited fearfulness. This oracle augurs that you will move gracefully through any negativity, leaving it behind you. Any mud being slung your way is not going to stick. Keep your sense of inner dignity intact. Do not make yourself smaller to placate the fear, hate or anger in another's heart. Take pride in who you are. Be proud to be you and to have this gift of a human life. Live your path with the full knowledge that you are meant to do so according to your own freewill.

233

Confetti

Maybe you sense it, or maybe it's the last thing you can imagine feeling right now, but either way a cause for celebration is imminent. To encourage yourself to enter into the party spirit, consider how you might enter into a pleasurable state of mind. There is always so much to do, but there are also times when energy is best spent in playfulness. This is perhaps the most enjoyable task of spiritual discipline you are ever going to be given, so if it resonates with you, why not relish it? Acknowledge the successes of others with peace in your heart, knowing that your own successes are well deserved. If you are still waiting for acknowledgement to come your way, this oracle confirms you shall receive it and perhaps sooner than you expect. Prepare to party.

234

Circus of Love

Love has its own wild ways that are brilliant, instinctive and often cannot be grasped by the mind. So, trust what your heart loves and is moved by and what compels it to open more fully to life and love. With this, all sorts of strange wonderfulness, creative chaos and bold colour shall find its way onto your path. Your life may begin to feel like a circus, but is there a better circus than the circus of love? If you have been struggling in matters of the heart, this oracle indicates a heart healing is happening. Your experience of love is about to become more vibrant, exciting and playful - perhaps even unconventional. It indicates that a love affair with a person, place or thing is going to begin or deepen. It's time to let yourself be swept off your feet.

235

The False Enchantment

In our modern world, there is an abundance of artificial light - both actual and symbolic. The false light promises so much and delivers so little. The false light is a siren song, a promise of whatever it is that you feel you cannot have, unless you compromise your integrity to get it. There is only one lesson to be learned through the false enchantment, no matter what circumstances surround it. The lesson is that what was obtained was not worth the price you paid for it. No matter how much you believed it would be otherwise, it simply will not be worthwhile. Do not begin the slippery slope of bargaining away your self-esteem. Say 'no' to the mind becoming confused and needy about something that is supposedly too good to miss. The sanctity of your inner being is priceless. Guard it carefully.

236

It's Your Move

The Universe is waiting for you to make your move. There are times when it's wise to wait for the way to be shown. There are times when you need to choose. It's as if the Universe is asking what you want and what you are willing to open up to. Don't waste a golden opportunity with such a receptive audience! Go into your heart and rummage around a little. Ask for what you want and express what is in your heart. Have a candid chat with the Universe, as if you are hanging out with your best friend. You don't need to instruct the Universe on the details or method of delivery. It's really about being courageous enough to open up and speak your truth. Don't be shy about expressing your feelings, your dreams and your desires. It doesn't need to be complicated. It just needs to be honest. It's a perfect time to set something in motion.

237 The Brilliant Simplicity of Your Heart

When the mind is in pain, things seem more complicated than they are. The heart is able to see with simplicity. This oracle suggests that the best way through the most apparently complex issues is often the simplest. Simplicity can be the approach that takes a single step and then pauses to reassess. Simplicity can be to focus on a common purpose, or to step back and take a breath to gather and ground yourself. It is suggested that - even if just for now - you drop the complex explanations, justifications and interpretations. Sometimes, the simple truth is fairly obvious. Don't dismiss it for being so! Take some time to settle into the simple truth of your heart and allow it to inform your approach and decisions.

238

Good Fortune

Luck isn't just for the lucky! Luck is a field of goodness, attracted to a certain type of mindset. It is an attitude, a belief that life wants to help you, and has the infinite power and creative imagination to do just that in endless ways. Attracting luck means being open to the genius of life, which works itself out perfectly, bringing benefits again and again. This oracle suggests that the Universe is handing you a golden ticket - a lucky break, a positive change in fortune that is in your stars and was always meant for you. Your good fortune and blessings can inspire and assist others, too. Feel the gratitude and the joy of your win, so that you may become so attractive to this energy that it wants to take up permanent residence in your life.

239 The Time of Your Life

There are times when our wishes - and the need for control - must give way for a larger plan to unfold in our lives. It is helpful to remember that, even though life may seem to be working against you in such moments, it is not. It may be that you need to adjust your attitude or expectations - from a place of trust - so that you can see the blessing being offered to you. The guiding hand of fate may close a door in your face! Yet the right doors will open at the right time. If there is pain now, trust that it is there so you avoid greater suffering later. You may sense instability or that things are going to change, and you'd be right. The more you trust in the process, the more you'll recognise that the Universe is working with you. If you allow it, it will show you the time of your life.

240 Plug into Your Power

Without access to your power, you lack the energy needed to follow through on your intuitions, take meaningful action, establish clear boundaries and remain courageously true to yourself, even if others misunderstand. Power can be misused when it is a tool of the ego. A sign that ego is taking over is that one's principles are manipulated or distorted in order to control others. When power is in service to the soul it is directed toward holding space for the authentic self. It is unconcerned about what anyone else is doing (or not doing). Where you once held back, your capacity to conquer situations increases when you plug into your power at a soul level. You are fast approaching a growth edge for your soul. This holds the potential to free you from past constraints and opens you up to a more joyful and fulfilling way of being. Give up attempts to control life, or anyone else, and direct your energies toward inner growth. There is something good and important that can happen for you now.

241

Alchemy of Acceptance

Far from condemning you to remain stuck in a situation, acceptance empowers you to move through the experience, uncovering opportunities for healing and growth that would otherwise have remained hidden. In any challenging set of circumstances, you can be sure that your soul is orchestrating your best path to a resolution that increases your spiritual fulfilment. You are strong enough to handle the honest acknowledgement that a situation is less than ideal. This oracle advises that you soften your heart and loosen your grip on what you want to achieve. The Universe is working with you. Stay committed to the path but also accept what is happening right now. A way through will be made available to you. You have more power to change things than you realise, and as you let go, you'll come to understand that the Universe is already sorting out your life circumstances for your benefit.

242 The Key to Your Purpose is You

To manifest your divine destiny and highest purpose, figure out who you really are, beneath the layers of conditioning, and then be that self as fully as you dare to be. Seek resonance and authenticity, rather than conditioned expectations about how things should be, and you will naturally gravitate to people, places and energies that will support you in being your bright, true spirit. You have no need to compare yourself to any other. Nor do you need to impose your will upon the mysterious workings of life. You are a unique child of the Universe with a special path and destiny to fulfil. Much goodness can come of honouring this truth. No-one else can assume your role and neither should you assume, control or direct the role of another. Live and let live. You will make a helpful contribution toward a brighter future for humanity and you won't miss a thing that is meant for you.

243

Question the Mass Viewpoint

Take the time to question and reflect upon what really means something to you. Otherwise, you're likely to be moved by the values that others seek to impose upon you. Those values may not mean anything to you at a deeper level, yet you'll be afraid to step outside of what others say is safe or true. Without pausing to reflect on your personal values, you will miss an opportunity to stand for what matters to your soul - living life in a way that really nourishes you and brings you a deep sense of satisfaction, healing and awakening. In the privacy of your own heart, question the values that you have been given. Decide for yourself what matters to you and what, in your heart, you truly believe. Live from that place and you'll truly live.

244

Your Power to Love Yourself

The only people who have the power to condemn you, steal your joy, and make you feel bad about who you are, are those you permit to do so. At any moment, you have the choice to liberate yourself from fearful or negative influences by deciding that you shall love yourself and commit unconditionally to being good to yourself, so that you can live in a way that honours what really matters to your heart. When you love yourself in this way, the Universe's capacity to help you increases radically. You'll find that what you need finds its way to you with far less obstruction. Your path may not look like that of any other, but when you truly love yourself, you don't need to compare. You can simply appreciate the differences, wonder at the infinite variety of soul paths available, and live your life. Know that you have the capacity to love and are truly worthy of being loved.

245

Veiled Destiny

Having no idea about where you are headed can be helpful, from a spiritual perspective. It helps you develop unconditional trust in the guiding wisdom of the Universe. It helps you stay focused on what you need to do right now, rather than getting so excited about the future, you become distracted from the work at hand, unwittingly slowing down your progress, and delaying the very future that you wish to draw closer to you. At other times, it is helpful to understand something from a bigger perspective and to see how what you are currently working on is going to assist your ultimate fulfilment. Trust that when you need to know something, the Universe will get the awareness to you. Trust what you sense, and trust in what you cannot yet know. Both are working toward your greater good.

246 Lighten the Heart to Find the Easier Way

Your beautiful heart has carried quite the burden of grief, suffering and sadness, not to mention anger and fear at various times. Your heart is beautiful and empowered and is doing a wonderful job as a loving instrument of your soul. It also needs a holiday now and then, to tune into its natural state - which is joy. To connect to that which evokes laughter, open your heart to the silly and wonderfully ridiculous side of life. It is highly recommended, not only now but as a regular practice of intentional joyfulness. This is not about being contrived or forcing laughter. It is about exploring ways to be in tune with your capacity for delight more often. It's a rather sad state of affairs in this world. Sometimes we take things far too seriously and sometimes very important things are dismissed altogether. Honest, joyful, good-natured and appreciative humour can do so much for so many. Take delight in your joyful spirit.

247 Peace Offering from the Universe

The Universe is offering a hand of friendship. You've been working hard. Even in your fatigue and exhaustion, you are still devoted to your path. It's time for the brightness of life to fill your heart and chase away the shadows of the past. You'll need your inner strength to give yourself permission to switch off, without plugging into guilt or anxiety for doing so. Be like the builder who after a full day's work, accepts that it is time to put down the tools for the day. Allow yourself some playtime and more peace, and you'll find it easier to accept that the Universe wants to be at play in your life in a more peaceful way, too.

248

Obscured View

During the journey, your view is rarely as clear as the one defining glimpse of the grander plan or purpose that we have at inception, or sometimes at the closure, of a cycle in our life. You can trust in the Universe and the guiding hand of your soul to help you along those twists and turns in the path where, in order to actually take the journey, you had to give up your eagle-eye view of the bigger picture. Trust that there is a team of helpers who have also seen the fuller vision and know your part in the plan. They are working with you, to ensure a successful outcome for all. When your view is obscured, your trust needs to be greater. In time you'll be able to see from a bigger perspective again. For now, commit to the details of your journey and know that a greater hand is guiding your process.

249

Asking for Help

The act of asking for support is not always so simple! The mind often dismisses such a notion as fanciful rather than practical. Perhaps the pain of having your needs rejected in the past has been so devastating that you have decided to be without needs, becoming self-sufficient, therefore not allowing for healthy vulnerability. Perhaps you may be afraid of becoming a burden to spirit, believing that our vast Universe would find your problems too much to deal with. The Universe has great power and desire to help all beings. Getting in the habit of aligning with that power and giving full permission for its grace to enter your world, makes the way easier for everyone. This oracle says that there is help wanting to make its way to you. It makes sense to invite the unconditionally loving and helpful wisdom into your world now. Relief shall arise as you do so.

250 Nourishing Carnelian

Carnelian is a warming, orange-red crystal with nourishing, strengthening and vitalising qualities. The spirit of this crystal brings a message to you. Consider what it is to truly nourish yourself on all levels - body, mind and soul. Much of what mass consciousness produces is based in fear and tends to generate the same. It is unlikely to nourish and strengthen anything other than one's ego. When you choose to sustain your heart and soul on healthier and more nurturing fare, your emotions become more settled, your body stronger, and your mind clearer. When your soul has more grip over your state of being than your ego does, your life path opens up with more joy and empowerment. What could feed your soul right now? You are allowed to choose to take in what will support you and pass on what will not.

251

Safe to be Seen

When someone has the courage to stand in the truth of their light and be visible in doing so (coming out of the spiritual closet, so to speak), there will be those that love and respect them for doing so, and others who cannot. Being increasingly visible can give rise to a sense of empowerment, but also feeling exposed. Remember that you are in possession of your own soul. No other person can ever own you. You have the right to set boundaries and to speak your truth freely, without seeking to override the freewill of others. Allowing yourself to be seen does not imply that another has any right to intrude or impose their view upon you. You can protect yourself in a field of spiritual grace and maintain a strong, private, inner spiritual connection at all times to sustain and support you. It is safe for you to be seen, even to stand out from the crowd.

252

Do Not Fear the Storm

The storms of nature can be intimidating and awe-inspiring. They have a powerful cleansing effect, releasing built-up energies, generating vitality and refreshment. However, when you are in the storm itself - especially if it is intense - you may fear its power, and question whether what you have treasured shall be swept away in its potential fury. Sometimes it can be hard to know what the Universe has in store for us, and why. All we can know is that it is directed toward our spiritual growth and we can move with it in trust, learning as we go. When things get a bit wild in your life, or in your mind, come back to the eye of the storm, the still place in the centre that recognises the fluctuations happening around you. Once they pass, there will be clarity and peace to proceed. Believe it or not, you are being blessed, and peace shall return.

253 Divine Lion

It is possible to be so inspired and on fire with soulful passion for an idea or vision, that it becomes more powerful in effect - on your body, mind and soul - than your fears. Whilst you have no need to control the behaviour of others - to each their own - you do have the right to reject the disparagement, disrespect and the attempts to control or manipulate you. The divine lion within your heart is dignified and courageous. It needs to be free to live with a sense of self-worth and self-respect, and to pursue its instincts toward growth and expansion. The divine lion needs to assume wise leadership within your being and your life. Additionally, if called to do so, perhaps for others in one's community, too. Be humble, but do not play small.

254

Setting Down the Load

We can become so used to holding on to our worries that it starts to feel natural to do so - and for an empath, that can include the worries of other people, too. It isn't until something happens to free us from this weight, that we realise how much easier our life flows when we don't hold on so tightly. Fear can have us reactively holding on to the very thing that is going to drown us, whilst trying to convince us that it is our life raft. As you loosen your grip and regain the energy you were losing in the process, you'll find that certain elements remain in your life effortlessly, whilst others that are no longer meant to be, fall gently away. Trust in the goodness of life so that you can let this happen. An easier path awaits you.

255 Invitation to the Banquet

You have freewill, so even when you sense the Universe asking you to let go of something or someone, you don't have to do so. Ultimately, it is exhausting and counterproductive to hold on to what needs to end. Nevertheless, the Universe respects us and allows us to learn and grow through our experiences and at our own pace. It can be helpful to remember that when we are asked to hand over the scraps that we have come to believe are our only treasures, it is so that we can be granted a true feast for the soul. You can truly acknowledge the value in what you have cherished and realise that the heart may need the freedom to move on. It is safe to let go, to process your feelings and then come to a place of peace and receptiveness. This oracle encourages you to make room for the goodness seeking access into your world.

256 From Poison to Purification

There are more poisons in the world at this time than ever before. There is also more compassion, more opportunities for healing and a greater possibility for making genuine, substantial spiritual growth. Purification happens most readily when there is relaxation and surrender. If there is resistance, then the process becomes more difficult. This oracle brings glad tidings of protection, and intervention to become free from harmful situations, substances and influences. Follow your hunches and seek the light that brings peace to your heart and mind. Be unafraid to do some significant clearing within you and around you, in all areas of your life. The Universe is actively working with you to bring you to a happier and healthier state of being.

257

Grace for the Grand Gesture

In a way, there is no such thing as a small step. Every step on the path is important, accumulating to create progress. However, there are times when a little more oomph is needed to break free from a holding pattern and access a new, more expansive, luminous, protected and inspired reality. This oracle indicates that you have capacity to take such a leap. It also indicates that at a spiritual level, you have been empowered to take a significant step, so that your path stays in alignment with your destiny. Tune into your heart and consider what you have been putting off, what it is that you need, and what will genuinely support you. Consider the steps you have been longing for but have not been ready to take. This oracle encourages you to reconsider your readiness now.

258 Bumbling Holds the Potential for Brilliance

If you have taken leaps of faith in the past and landed flat on your face rather than gracefully on your toes, leave that memory behind you now. So, your skilfulness didn't quite match your courage at the time. That's okay. In fact, it was rather daring of you! Nothing much happens without the inspired, daring and yet inelegant scrambles for new ground from time to time. Everything you have experienced in your life has helped you become the person that you are today, different to the person you have previously been. The Universe is urging you on. You may worry that you will repeat past failures. But there have been no actual failures, only growth experiences. Trust what you've learned and keep bumbling along in your beautiful, brilliant way.

259

Listen to Your Heart

The knowing of the heart cuts through the confusion of the mind. When the heart recognises a truth, you just know - even if there is every logical reason why the truth should be otherwise. The heart senses the truth of a situation in an instant, whereas the mind argues convincingly for one side and then for the exact opposite, ending up in confusion. The mind is a valuable asset, but if we allow it to run roughshod over the truths of the heart, we can miss so much and take a far longer time to get where we need to be. There is something in your life that your heart just knows, even if your mind questions it. Save yourself from unnecessary drama and suffering. Listen to your heart.

260

Heart Opening

Purification often happens when the heart is opening further, awakening to a new level of expansive presence. Purification may involve revisiting old wounds. As the heart outgrows the old ways, those stuck energies are flushed out of body, mind and soul. This doesn't necessarily feel good at the time. Like any detoxification, it can be uncomfortable before it gets better. That's putting it nicely. It might feel like a damn nightmare! If it's happening, it is because you are capable of going through it and transforming positively through the process. Once the drama of your past wounds starts to clear and settle, your heart will have an increased spaciousness and capacity for blissful love, and a powerful presence. If this is happening, stay with it. You are not regressing. You are healing. Your heart knows what it is doing. Trust in a deeper wisdom guiding your path.

261

Soul Speak

Your authentic voice is like no other. This is why it can take some time to find it. In a way, it finds you when you create the space, patience and non-judgement required for it to rise up from the depths of your being. This voice of the soul may not always be soft, but in its own way, it will always be loving. You can be inspired by the voices of others, but there is wisdom in avoiding comparison. Your voice is meant to be different, to be unique, and to be your own. The voice yearns for expression, as that is its nature. Authentic expression is not about conversion, coercion or manipulation. It is the sharing of an experience. When you offer a communication that comes from your heart, without agenda, your capacity to manifest your life path increases and your ability to empower others through your voice, grows too. Express your soul.

262

Angel of Mercy

Every now and then, even the most saintly amongst us will have less-than-stellar moments. If we maintain a sense of humour in the face of such moments, then they can help us to stay humble and compassionate. From such a perspective, these stuff-ups are therefore very helpful. In our less skilful moments however, we might also cause harm to another, even if we did not start out with such an intention. The quality of mercy softens the repercussions of our actions and in the face of genuine contrition, often provides a full pardon. You are allowed to be human. You are doing your best. Divine mercy helps to bridge the gap when our efforts fall short of the mark. Let yourself, and others, off the hook of judgement. From the heart, ask for the sacred blessings of mercy to touch all in need and know that everything is going to be okay.

263

Giving Up Guilt

Your life path will unfold in whatever way best serves your growth. Upon occasion, that will involve facing some challenges. Perhaps you are particularly adept at transforming adversity into success and thrive in such moments. Perhaps you are more intimidated than excited by challenge. Even if you believe the toughest challenges are the only way to bring out the best in you, there is benefit for every soul to have some lightness of spirit and experience gentleness at times. This oracle suggests that you can experience much more of this if you decide to stop being so hard on yourself. Give up guilt and you'll gain access to grace.

264 Welcome Relief

Consciously choosing to surrender one's concerns and to genuinely ask a higher wisdom to provide the way for a resolution, brings tremendous relief, relaxation and peace. To not have to have all the answers, or always be in control, and for everything to still work out in your world - even in better ways than you could have imagined - engenders trust. If you are feeling betrayed, frightened or confused, then remember that although the mind is powerful, it needs regular and compassionate reminders that it is not privy to the workings of the entire Universe. Nor does it need to be, for your affairs to work out wonderfully. This oracle says that the intricate workings of a higher plan are at play in your life, even now.

265 You are Not Crazy to Trust the Universe

The key purpose of higher is loving evolution – but there are times when this is hard to believe. Intellectually, you may know the Universe loves you and is always helping you. Emotionally, you may feel insecure, uncertain or challenged by what is happening and wish life was other than it is. Right now, you are growing. Sometimes growth entails suffering. We may not enjoy every phase of the process and we may not be sure what it is we are supposed to be learning but when we stay with the process all of that changes. Even the most faithful of us wonder if we are foolish to trust in the Universe, at times. We may feel as though we are deluding ourselves. Then healing comes, suffering goes, and faith is affirmed. It may be easier to trust next time. You may be a little crazy (in a good way). But you are not crazy to trust the Universe.

266

Sensitive Soul

Sensitivity can feel like a burden when one is suffering emotional and psychological anguish. The pain is felt so much more. Yet, exquisite sensitivity is necessary for conscious communication with the beautiful spiritual realms. The alternative of becoming numb would be like draining all art, colour and music from the world. This oracle brings guidance that you can hold a safe space for your sensitivity. It indicates an awakening of greater perception and an adjustment process where you may feel, for a time, more sensitive to incoming impressions. Your heightened capacity for feeling may not always be pleasant, but it is an asset endowing you with an excellent detector for ego masquerading as something it's not. Do not begrudge it. It is the seat of so much wisdom.

267

Interiority

Discernment is an ability to sense purity, truth and love from that which appears, believes or deceptively claims to be other than it is. This does not mean that you must assume an attitude of suspicion or distrust. It does mean that it is wise to trust what you feel and sense beneath the surface of things, especially when it appears to run contrary to popular opinion or what is claimed. The more stark the contrast between what you feel and what is being presented, the more you should pay attention. This is not about feeling vindicated in judging another. Discernment is not fancy spiritual terminology for permission to expose and criticise another person. It is about tuning in to what you intuitively sense, rather than dismissing it or negatively indulging in it. You'll need to access your interiority - your inner being - to cut through illusion and judgement, and to sense what it is that your wise self wants you to notice. If you are using discernment, as opposed to judging, then you will learn a little more about yourself through the process rather than fixating on why so-and-so isn't all he or she is cracked up to be. You gain a helpful insight and adjust your course accordingly. This oracle asks you to look more deeply and feel for the truth as your inner being senses it.

268 Abundant Grace and Precious Opportunities

When you believe in abundant grace, there is no need to hold on to the blessings that are flowing because there is no fear that they will stop. There is a belief in constant evolution and expansion, continual growth and unlimited supply. It is a beautiful belief system that heals greed, by answering the belief in lack that lies beneath it. Yet one needs to take care that this belief system doesn't generate complacency or lack of regard for the value of opportunities given, or for the precious time allotted to us for this unique lifetime of ours. If you believe in reincarnation, you can acknowledge that your soul will never experience this exact lifetime again. There is so much that you can choose to do with your life. What would you like to choose for yourself? Commit to your life with awareness of the possibilities and the precious time you have been given. Do not squander precious hours on things that diminish the love in your heart.

269 Don't Override Higher Wisdom

Take care that your positive intentions remain in harmony with a higher wisdom rather than your own - or any other person's - opinion. If you believe that human opinion is the determinant of who should be healed, and how and when, you will compromise your ability to be a surrendered and effective channel for light on this planet. Even if another accuses you of selfishness, you will be guided when, where and how to be of assistance. Do only what you genuinely feel guided to do from a place of fearlessness, inspiration and love. No matter how spiritually it may be dressed up to appear, all else is the working of ego, and will not bring you the beautiful outcome you seek.

270

Alchemical Shift

Alchemy is the transformation that cannot be undone - the irreversible shift from one state or stage of being into an entirely different one. Like the caterpillar becoming the butterfly, there are certain stages on one's spiritual journey where you outgrow what you have been and mature into the next evolution of your true self. On the surface, alchemy seems improbable at best, or even impossible. It doesn't make sense. At a deeper level, there is an intelligence guiding the process that has a brilliant capacity to bring the true inner potential into a most unexpectedly beautiful higher expression. This oracle speaks of a transformation that is so profound it can never be undone. The caterpillar knows how to become the butterfly, even if it cannot know that it will become one. Place your faith in the inner guiding intelligence that is growing you into what you must be.

271

Empowered Service

We can have beautiful dreams in our hearts to be of assistance, to serve a higher cause and shine light in this world. Such aspirations ought to be nurtured and respected. However, there is always that sometimes pesky, yet always protective and ultimately helpful matter of divine timing. We will go through phases of building foundations, developing new skills and learning lessons that prepare us for taking a step up, and then learning how to traverse the higher levels of the spiritual path. Until we are ready to take yet another step, and so on. This oracle speaks of progress being made on the path, with new opportunities to serve emerging in due course. Whatever is in your heart, you shall be empowered to do.

272

Magnetic Attraction

There is a spiritual web of connectivity that links all phenomena. That connective intelligence attracts you toward, and towards you, what is needed. As you let go of past experiences of rejection, perceived failure and the belief that you have to control how things happen rather than trusting, your capacity to consciously play in the field of magnetic attraction increases exponentially. There is an exquisite intelligence to divine design, a way for every possible beauty to emerge, even out of what seems to be a problem. We cannot ever really fathom its grace from a human point of view. Nevertheless, we are always welcomed into its divine embrace. Let the attractive power of your heart, magnetise what you wish to experience in your world with relaxed, trusting gratitude.

273 Connection to Higher Worlds

How we connect spiritually has a high degree of variability. The method for connection is less important than its effect - clearing the mind of distortions such as negative emotions and fixed opinions, so that something truer and deeper may be perceived. This oracle encourages you to seek out connection to the beautiful higher worlds of love, light and wisdom. It encourages you to actively ask for their blessings in your life. You'll be able to recognise the presence of higher guidance by the feeling it evokes within you. It will change your emotional and mental state, bringing you into a place of clarity and peaceful healing. You will feel satisfied that your question has been answered until a new question arises. As you build your beautiful relationship with the loving spiritual guardians that watch over all of humanity, you'll find your ability to connect happens more readily and tends to endure. If you've been wanting to make such contact or wonder if it is already happening, this oracle is a confirmation.

274 The Real, Real World

Have you ever been told that you need to live in the real world? Or maybe you secretly fear that whilst you love the visions you have, they are not something that could ever manifest in the real world. What is the real world? Turns out, it's not so real after all. There is more for you to be, do, receive and share. Allow your inner rebel to emerge and guide you on the path that fills you with enough passion that you are willing to work and be devoted to it. The real world is the world that you relate to from an empowered connection with your innermost being. It is not accessed through conformity or convention. The door to it opens when you are willing to be real with yourself. No-one else can decide or dictate that for you. The real world is the one that is true for the real you.

275

Deflection of Projection

Psychological projection is the effort of the wounded ego to avoid its pain by imagining (often most convincingly, yet not truthfully) that the source of pain is all about some other person. People will often give opinions very decidedly about others they have never personally met and know nothing about. This is projection at work. Then there are the projections from those we are in personal relationship with. These can become so powerful over time that we begin to believe in what others want us to be rather than what we deeply know ourselves to be. If you are on the receiving end of such a phenomenon, you may feel compelled to meet that person's expectations. Yet taking the rap for another's ego wounds continues the drama of suffering for both of you. The only permission you ever need to claim, live, respect and love your real self, is your own.

276

Cosmic Breadcrumbs

Although we may want a conclusive answer to a larger issue, all we really need to know in any moment is what to do next. By tuning into your feelings and trusting your intuition rather than becoming caught up in logic, you'll sense the next step that feels best for you. Proceeding one step at a time is like following a line of breadcrumbs along a great winding path, to help you find your way. The journey may be too magnificent to handle all at once. It's like asking someone for directions and twenty minutes later they are still explaining! You'd never remember it all! However, it would be helpful to be given just enough to get you to the next checkpoint. Even when your current situation seems confusing, this oracle advises that you shall find your way. Tune in and take it one step at a time. You are being led by wisdom greater than your own.

277

Freewill and Destiny

With freewill, your destiny can unfold with amazing creative possibilities. Freewill allows you to choose the extent of your commitment, courage, the free-spirited silliness that creates joy, and the authentic presence that allows for your emotional healing and psychological insight. You get to choose what to make a priority in your life, and what to cast aside. Your journey will be a vastly different experience for you depending on these choices, and you get to revise your choices whenever you wish. Life knows the preordained encounters, connections and timing that need to happen for the greater plan to unfold - life knows where you are headed. You have a lot of room to choose, play and co-create with life. For today, what do you choose?

278

Relief and Repair

When given adequate rest and spaciousness, your body, mind and soul know how to heal. Inspiration and adventure are important facets of an exciting and fulfilling life journey. They open us to life's possibilities. Like a delicious meal from an unfamiliar cuisine, they can usher in new pleasures. Without the space and time to digest and integrate, the deeper value of those experiences can be lost. An addictive state of endless exploration may emerge until the inner being cries out, needing to ground, settle, and reflect. If such needs are not answered, one's wellbeing on all levels is eventually the cost. You've been taking a lot in. Give yourself time to process and integrate it. Then you'll be ready for another adventure, wiser for the experiences you've already had.

279 The Boundaries of Personal Responsibility

Fear is sticky and contagious. It can infiltrate our best intentions and courageous actions when we allow ourselves to take the critical remark of another to heart. You may wonder what you have done to attract a situation into your life. Conscious people can unintentionally undermine their own progress by taking inappropriate responsibility for other people's actions. Being responsible for your own responses is appropriate. Assuming that the actions of another are your own doing is not. Take care not to collude in such a fearful delusion. Do not agree that it is appropriate behaviour for another to blame you for their pain. Let your compassion be fierce enough that you will not play the victim to another's point of view. You will then protect all from the insidious games of ego.

280 Soft Intervention

Love, perhaps especially in its most gentle forms, can trigger the release of stored pain. If you have become accustomed to toughness, the unexpected appearance of gentleness is disarmingly powerful and can be an astonishing and welcomed alternative. When one has been struggling for a long time and have perhaps concluded that this is just the way life is, accepting and trusting in a gentler way can take some time and courage. This oracle foretells a gentle intervention, a softness that is more powerful than force and will accomplish far more for all. Open your heart and mind to it. There are better times ahead.

281

Passionate Energy

When there is passion in your heart, you will naturally dedicate yourself with an intensity and discipline that may otherwise elude you. Passion is love activated. It moves you from within and empowers you to act in ways that you would not otherwise dare to consider. It gives you strength and generates ability to accomplish things you might not have dreamed were possible. Great things happen when wild dreamers let their love loose in the world. However, with great passion, there can also be great pain. Take time to nurture your heart through setbacks and challenges, with knowing they are part of the journey. If it seems like all is lost, then you are not at the final chapter. Let your passion motivate you, rather than burn you out. Be committed, be balanced, be optimistic.

282

From Lemons to Lemonade

Healthy self-esteem tends to attract us to that which uplifts, assists and inspires. Sometimes, however, a wound within unconsciously attracts us toward that which is lowering in vibration. Such experiences do not feel good, but they can be the motivational push we need to break free from such circumstances once and for all, because we simply cannot bear to feel that way anymore! There's nothing wrong with lemons, especially when you understand that, through your inner healing, you have the choice to transform sour fruit into sweet effect. In India, it is taught that if the soul had a flavour, it would be sweet. Find a way to be sweeter, kinder and gentler with yourself. This is not indulgence. It is switching the harshness of a painful ego sting for the enlightening sweetness of soul.

283

Speaking Your Frequency

Your voice and your words are immediate ways to elevate, or lower, your frequency of being. Higher frequency beings feel better and attract spiritual intervention more easily - not because higher frequency is better, only because its nature is openness and love. When you find yourself dwelling on the negative, switch it up. Adjust your attitude. Speak about yourself and your life differently. For every negative, there is a positive reframe that is authentic and helpful. Use your words to grow good feelings in your heart and your world. Acknowledge your pain when you need to, but also acknowledge your intention and capacity to grow through it. You have the right and the spiritual responsibility, to choose which of the many and varied voices in this world you allow to enter, and remain, within you.

284

Daring Rebirth

It takes daring to imagine a new life and willingness to allow yourself to live in a different way. The truth can have many different versions and expressions, some fearful, others free. Rebirth speaks of a new you - a you that is truthful, emotionally authentic, and yet more vibrant and free. The need for daring is because the prospect of no longer living as the familiar version of yourself can be unfathomable to the mind. What would you be on the other side of the fear, shame, guilt, anger or other emotional binds that you need to release for rebirth to take place? What would your life be like? This oracle comes to you with the opportunity to confront and overcome something which has tied you to a version of yourself that is incompatible with where your life is now heading. Your rebirth can be so daring that you will feel as though you are living an entirely different life within this lifetime. Although it may not be easy, what you are giving up will not be a cause for regret.

285

Feeling Secure Spiritually

Humans equate familiarity and predictability with security. However, change is a constant part of life. Relying on things to remain the same is not a particularly helpful approach for feeling secure. There is another way to experience a sense of inner security that can help you feel safe and grounded whilst life does its unending backflips and spontaneous upheavals. The security comes from knowing that life - despite appearances to the contrary - is not utterly random. There is a working of a greater wisdom beneath all appearances. Destiny is not only a destination. It is a living process that evokes growth and spiritual evolution. You might not be able to rely on predictability in your life, but you can rely on the compassionate goodness that will support you through even the most unexpected or unwanted experiences. There is somewhere safe for you to rest, right now. Seek out that spiritual ground and know peace.

286

Glittering Lure of the Future

Creative types tend to be future-oriented and inspired by what could be. Innovation can be healthy and helpful. There is also wisdom in choosing to nurture, protect and cultivate what already exists and has value to the heart. When an idea is brilliant, but a little ahead of its time, it should not be cast aside, only given time to develop - and for the rest of the world to catch up to it. Perhaps you have a situation that needs an answer, and you believe that out there, somewhere, you shall find it, when in actuality, you already have the information or connections you need. This oracle speaks of a positive future that begins now, with tuning into the valuable assets already at your disposal. There's no need to get too far ahead of yourself. Look to what is already with you and you'll find what you need. Be inspired by possibility whilst you find what you need in the here and now.

287

Permission for Pleasure

The more the natural need for pleasure, delight, ecstasy and enjoyment are denied, the more addictive and potentially damaging our pursuit of pleasure becomes. We then think that pleasure is the problem, but the culprit is the denial as it forces us into an unnatural relationship with our healthy needs. Knowing that you'll have regular access to genuine, natural pleasure is a way to bear the inevitable pains of life. Many people have been shamed for yearning and expressing pleasure. There can be confusion, uncertainty and tension around letting go. Yet when there is a yearning for pleasure, your inner self is letting you know that you're too tightly wound up. Healthy pleasure creates energy, addictive approaches to pleasure deplete your life force and freewill, often triggering a spiral of indulgence followed by harsh denial and negative emotions. From self-loathing to self-love, this oracle guides you to play with sacred pleasure as a way to love yourself and to love life.

288

Power of Being an Encourager

Goodwill toward others - and oneself - is a type of spiritual power that benefits and protects you from negativity and harm, whilst empowering others to take their journey. It plugs you into a network of luminous spiritual guardians and helps attract positive energy and opportunities to you. Goodwill is generated by how you feel inside, and the attitude that you cultivate toward others. When you know you have value, it is easy to recognise the value in another. When you feel encouraged by the Universe, it is easy to encourage others. As you put out support, encouragement and goodwill for the success of all, this energy is amplified and returned to you. There is no need to compete or to feel fear of missing out. Trust in your rightful divine inheritance and that you can receive without diminishment of what is available to another. Focus on how good you feel within yourself and how you want the best for all. Encourage, to attract your rightful success.

289

Sacred Revolution

There are times when gentle evolution is insufficient to dislodge a pattern stuck in the soul. More extreme spiritual intervention is required. The dark goddess may stomp into your life, wearing her lotus-flower embossed combat boots, and kick you out of the nest so that you realise you can fly. She may rip the life raft out of your hands, causing you to splutter temporarily until you stand up and realise you can walk safely out of the rampaging river. Or she may knock the control freak dominating your mind, on the head, and set up her own temporary divine dictatorship where she simply repeats, "Love yourself and let go," until you do just that. Something powerful is happening. You won't feel in control of it. Trust it.

290

Protection of Your Integrity

Integrity is intention, word and action in harmony. It creates inner security, confidence and self-esteem. It allows you to make choices without compromising yourself. Integrity is your anchor to self and authenticity. When you are in tune with this part of yourself, you know what you need to do (or not do). Integrity exists when a person cares enough about their impact on the lives of others that they are willing to make the tough calls, rather than taking the path that seems easiest. You are seeking to live in honest communion with your heart. As long as you are right with you, what anyone else has to say on the matter, is not your concern.

291 Manifestation Through Integrity

Integrity requires strength of character. Integrity refuses to go against one's inner values to suit the power plays of another. However, it doesn't make life harder. It brings honour, enjoyment and (eventually) inner peace, even if your mind challenges you over stepping away from an amazing opportunity that didn't feel right, no matter how many ways you tried to spin it. As your integrity grows stronger, your ability to attract more of what you need also strengthens. Instead of needing to chase after what you want, you stand still and draw the right people and opportunities to you. You naturally push away those that look good superficially but would have caused disturbance. Any perceived loss that comes from staying in integrity is a saving grace from far bigger problems. Continue to be true to yourself.

292 Unplug from Mass Conditioning

At some point on the spiritual path, you will realise that you need to unplug from mass conditioning. This is a liberating, exciting time, but it can be frightening too, as you are learning to stand on your own spiritual ground, supported by your inner knowing, authenticity and sense of value. It can be threatening to those who want to maintain control over you. They will resist your spiritual emancipation by trying to play on your weakness - such as labelling your behaviour as selfish or delusional - in order to undermine your growing self-confidence and make you more emotionally pliable. The loss of what you once considered supportive or loving can be staggering. Yet it is necessary if you are to experience the utter joy of truly being yourself, and loving and being loved from that place, without fear. You are not meant to be seeing the world as most others do. Trust your process and keep going.

293

From Homeless to Homecoming

To embrace your freedom requires courage. As you liberate yourself, you'll experience extraordinary gains, but you'll also encounter loss. The loss may include people, places or things to which you have become attached, and would have suffocated your soul. It can be a shock to discover the price of freedom. It is why, even with all the power of choice in the modern world, there are still so few individuals who are truly free. The path to freedom involves a type of temporary homelessness. You don't belong in the world you once knew, and you are travelling toward something that is yet to be. You may feel spiritually orphaned from society, even from your family and friends. When a wild animal has been wounded, it keeps on the move until it can find a safe place to rest and recover. Your instincts will guide you to do the same as you heal the wounds inflicted upon your soul by fear-based belief systems. While at times difficult, you are on a worthy journey with an ultimately happy resolution. Take comfort in your own courage and know that your freedom does not come at the cost of being alone forever. You shall connect again in a new way, with love and freedom to be as you are.

294

Deprogram to Reprogram

Deprogramming yourself from mass consciousness is a task of emotional and psychological self-liberation. It empowers your capacity to choose how you live, to know yourself, to be authentic and to feel in harmony with your heart. There will be a point where deprogramming will shift to reprogramming. Instead of fighting against what has been drummed into your body, mind and soul through fear, you will feel free to embrace more loving realities, new ideas and dare to make choices that put those new realities to the test. This is usually the time the more fearful amongst your connections will start rumbling about how you are 'living in a dream world'. What others say and believe about you is about them, not your reality. Part of your unplugging process involves reclaiming any power you have given away, so that the opinions of others no longer carry weight in your soul, only the truths of your own heart. Give your emerging self, and your emerging reality, all the time, energy and patience it needs to come to fruition.

295

From Avoidance to Awareness

Fear can make us do silly things. We step away from the thing we most need to look at closely to bring us clarity and peace, yet we are afraid that we may witness something terrible about ourselves. Perhaps we fear we are unlovable, unworthy or not a good enough person. Confronting a fear that is holding us back from seeing a situation clearly is a very helpful thing to do, provided it is done with wisdom. This wisdom may require asking for support so that we approach the issue when we are willing to see it for what it is and accept whatever decisions we need to make. More often than not the choices that arise from the confrontation bring relief and resolution rather than distress. Even if you generally think of yourself as a capable person, or even if you don't, you are more capable of dealing with your life circumstances than you are giving yourself credit for.

296 Protect Your Energy

Compassion for yourself and others is a source for your power and your protection. It energises and moves you to act for relief of another's plight, without taking on their suffering and draining yourself, becoming distraught or fatigued. If you have been judging yourself or another, then it is possible you have become enmeshed in their pain and have lost your compassion. If you are feeling used, exploited or taken advantage of in any way, this oracle advises you to summon your compassion for yourself and others. Give yourself permission to disengage from the drama and take care of your own needs first. An empty vessel cannot give anything to anyone. When you are on solid inner ground, you can then respond, rather than react, to what is happening around you, and choose your course of action with wisdom. Care for yourself now so that your natural joyfulness can return to your heart.

297

Self-Belief

Magnificent manifestations become possible when the human heart chooses to believe in oneself. Life rallies to strengthen and encourage that brave willingness to be alive and not give up on what matters to the soul. Despite heartbreak and disappointment, your beautiful heart desires deepening of love. Even through those passing moments of doubt or despair, you choose to continue. You have the spirit of the phoenix within your heart. Acknowledge the trials you have gone through in life - some have been considerable - yet, while wise to notice the consequent wounds that need your loving attention, it is also good to look for the light, to see how you have grown, to note that you are still here. Continue with your divinely defiant, sacred rebel belief in yourself. You are a marvellous creature.

298

Courage to Continue

Sometimes we just need to know that everything is going to be okay. We are willing to keep going, to do the work, to take risks, but part of us just needs some encouragement. Akin to the finish line slowly coming into view - we can see what's left to travel and we know we are going to accomplish what we set out to do. Keep love as your motivation. Let any feelings of hate, fear or any motivation other than love be released. You will have your pains, but you will move through them, grow wiser and continue successfully on your path, moving from strength to strength. If anyone or anything tries to stop you or block you, you shall garner your energies within your true self, become even more powerful, and win. Nothing will defeat you.

299 True Power Comes from What You Release

There is a misconception that power comes from what you gain - money, status, the ability to control circumstances in another's life, and so on. Yet our real power comes from within. Take care not to allow yourself to become an emotional hostage to another's misconception of power. Your power is concentrated in the courage of your heart, in refusing to allow hate, bitterness or vengeance take up permanent residence and instead regularly giving yourself whatever you need to be able to naturally come back to a heart space, oriented in love. Don't put yourself down. Don't take the actions of others personally, and do not accept any disrespectful behaviour. As you let go of ego and embrace your loving spiritual connection with the Universe, you can come to know deep and true power, based on wisdom and compassion.

300 Wise Choice, Fulfilling Commitment

An abundance of choice can create a struggle to commit. Often, the issue stems not from an unwillingness to make a commitment, but from the concern that one may not make the best choice. It is wise to take time in reflection, but not to douse one's inclinations with excessive caution. Remember that once you make a choice, another decision, and another, shall be required as the path unfolds. Rather than attempting to see too far into the future, consider what feels authentic, inspired and genuinely inviting at this moment. Sense the reality beneath the surface appeal and if you are willing to proceed, do so with a sense of curiosity and courage for what will be. You are capable of wise choices and commitment.

301

Rare Success

There are some unique creative offerings that are like rare and precious pearls. Many valuable creations can manifest swiftly, but some are truly labours of love, and require long-term commitment to nurture them into life. These exquisite creations are the sacred manifestations of rare success. These will stand the test of time to provide a sanctuary of comfort, encouragement and grace, for generations to come. Your soul is a precious pearl, a lifetime-long evolving creation of love and wisdom. This oracle brings you reassurance that you have the capacity for unusual creative offerings worth the effort required to bring them to life. Sometimes the need for immediate results has to be relinquished to the timing of a greater purpose. Stay true to your path, and do not be dissuaded if you are yet to see the results you had hoped. Continue to commit to, and trust in, your destiny.

302

Detachment and Desire

On the spiritual path, there is a time and place for detachment. The ability to step back and perceive from a neutral perspective can bring clarity. There is also a time to melt into sacred passion and allow the deep desires of the soul to motivate you to accomplish more than is otherwise possible. The path of fervent longing is not an easy one. Yet it is the path of the mystic willing to know unconditional, intimate union with spiritual truth, no matter where the journey leads. Mystics overcome great obstacles and succeed due to their enduring passion, while the more logic-driven scratch their heads and wonder how they managed to pull off what they did. Whether or not you relate to the mystical path, this oracle encourages you to find your true path by asking what moves you to work hardest for it. What does being you require of you? Your passions are fuel for your journey. Let them warm your heart and motivate your mind.

303

Play to Win

There are issues in our lives and in the world that need to change and be healed. The feminine wisdom within the human heart knows how to bring about healing change with love, playfulness, courage and dignity. The heart knows how to reach out and connect without harming another, offering rather than demanding. The notion that we can ignore our hearts and go against what we feel is right and true because society says so, is dangerous. It is no way to thrive. It is not even a way to survive. Often the way through the most serious and intense situations can be through finding the lighter spirit - not dismissing or mocking - but simply affirming the healing power that unconventional approaches of the heart can bring. With play, we can outsmart the ego and refuse to be subject to its rules. Tune into your heart and don't be afraid to have some fun.

304

Wonderful Wrangler

You can handle complicated situations with more finesse than most. You are encouraged to stay open to what is, and not turn away when the levels of chaos, creativity and unpredictability reach new heights! Don't allow your mind to talk you out of something before you really weigh up what you sense and how you feel. You have an ability to remain serenely engaged with the unfamiliar that is well above average. Once you get your bearings and sense the lay of the land, you will find a way to thrive, enjoy what you discover and experience the unexpected gift that life wants to send your way.

305

No More Self-Harm

If you interpret the behaviour of other people or circumstances beyond your control to indicate something negative about you, you will make yourself unnecessarily miserable. Work through whatever needs to be laid to rest, so that you can forgive yourself for whatever it is that you've been taking yourself to task over. You can learn from your past choices more easily if you stop punishing yourself whenever you feel that you've made a mistake. Even decisions that we once regretted can become the best learning experiences (and later on, fabulous dinner-party stories). Sometimes the only way to learn what we need to know is from what doesn't work out at the time. Be good to yourself. Have your own back.

306

Safeguard the Open Heart

You have a beautiful heart, and sometimes others cannot meet it on equal terms of openness, generosity and compassion. Their hearts may be too closed or afraid, due to past pain. That's okay. It's part of your life purpose to bring love into this world because people like this really need more of it in their lives. You never need to turn down the light of love in your heart, but you do deserve to safeguard and protect it. When fearful, angry people lash out in pain, trying to hurt others because they cannot get past their own hurt, do not make it about you. Reinforce your boundary and your beauty. Your heart knows how to love and protect you whilst holding compassion for the suffering others could be feeling. Give to yourself just as you give to the world - with kindness and generosity.

307

Good Guides Only

When seeking guidance in life, it is wise to apply careful selection criteria. This is obvious yet so easily forgotten in our sometimes-desperate desire for answers. If we accept guidance or influence from another, it is important to make sure they are the kind of person we aspire to be. You can learn from and be inspired by others, but you must stay true to yourself if you want to live a meaningful and enriching life. This oracle suggests that you take care not to allow anyone else's voice to become more important to you than the divine voice within. When good guidance is given, it will resonate faithfully with your own heart.

308

Worthy Friends

Those rare people who accept themselves unconditionally will be able to accept all parts of you unconditionally, too. Others, who struggle to accept themselves, may struggle to accept you - not because you are unworthy of such acceptance, but because they are still learning what it means to love unconditionally. We are all learning something, and such people are not going to be helped by further judgement. Nonetheless, you do need to remember that they may want you to conform to their opinions and to behave in a certain way, to remain in their favour. Maybe they think they are helping you in censoring you or advising you, but they are not. You won't help them or yourself by trying to be a different person. Be a worthy friend to yourself as well as others.

309

Dragonfly's Direction

Dragonflies are capable of the most astonishingly precise and rapid changes in direction. This oracle brings you a message from this soul totem. You have it within you to handle even dramatic changes in direction and remain true to your life path. Sometimes our path twists and turns, and we are amazed at the direction we end up heading in, as it is so different to what we once expected. Life is abundant with blessings - and difficulties - but if you are not happy with something, you have the power to change it. Whether this relates to a shift in mood or a radical change on your life path, you've got the power to accomplish it swiftly, and with absolute certainty. Have faith in your abilities.

310

Every Saint Has A Past

This oracle reminds you that happiness and freedom is your spiritual destiny, and you have not forsaken it by making mistakes in the past. If you have been holding yourself up to inhuman standards of perfection and then criticising yourself for falling short - or doing this to others - you are advised to stop such behaviour now. Perhaps you thought it would bring out the best in you, but constant criticism or driving for more is wearying to the soul that needs to balance movement and creativity with appreciation and gratitude for what is, resting in contentment. Don't break with the passionate pursuit of your dreams. Give yourself the nourishing gift of contentment too, so that your soul is sustained and sated, as well as inspired and motivated.

311

Magdalene

You are going to free yourself from a painful criticism or judgement held against you - perhaps by another or yourself. Human beings do not have the spiritual right to condemn each other or ourselves. Every human is here on Earth to learn to grow and every human will make mistakes along the way. You are realising that you can claim responsibility for yourself and your actions and make amends when it is appropriate to do so, from a place of dignity and respect. You are realising that you don't have to be perfect to be pure of heart and deserving of respect and kindness. You hold the spirit of Magdalene in your heart - dignity, courage and an inner compulsion to defy convention, seek out the truth and live it wholeheartedly.

312

Star Light, Star Bright

A subconscious fear of being judged or becoming the target of jealousy can cause us to shy away from being seen. There is a commonly held belief that being in the spotlight must mean that you think you are better than everyone else. There is a higher purpose in standing apart from the crowd and being seen. It can be about developing self-acceptance and self-confidence. You can become so comfortable in your own skin that you no longer hide who you are. Others may become less afraid to be themselves too because you have shown them that being cool is about being cool with who you are and refusing to be stereotyped by people with insufficient imagination. Don't let fear shut you down. You are bolder, brighter and bigger than that.

313

Home of the Heart

Finding intimate, soul-deep belonging begins with you reaching out, learning to love and care for yourself, and feeling at home within your own being. Give your heart permission to reveal to you the people, places and activities that generate a feeling of home. You are in a phase of transition in your life, casting off what is not true to your heart, in favour of what authentically belongs in your world. Sometimes the mind resists, thinking that if we let go of too much, we'll be left with nothing - and that it's better to hold on even if something isn't right. Such a belief makes it more difficult for you to find your way home. This is not about demanding perfection. It is about sensing authentic resonance. It's safe to trust your heart as it attracts into your world that which assists you and guides you into what is truly meant for you. Your beautiful heart deserves a real home.

314

Finch Soul Messenger

Finches can become beautifully coloured birds when they eat foods that nourish them. They can reveal their inner beauty but only when they have the correct nourishment to transform potential into expression. You have beautiful potential within you, and the ability to bring it to life in your world. To do so, you need to feed your soul the love and respect it requires to flourish. From the food you eat (taking a moment to bless any food with gratitude before you eat can help a lot), to the information you take in, to the voices in your head that you encourage or challenge - you are making choices to either nourish or deplete yourself. Finch spirit guide brings a prediction of happiness ahead, of fulfilment and self-expression. There is great joy and opportunity in your future to live a truly soulful and successful life. Nourish yourself to prepare for it.

315

She Saved Herself

Even if you feel uncertain about a challenge before you, believe in yourself. Help will be there when you need it, even if it is coming from unexpected quarters. Your inner resources hold the internal energies to attract the right, next step always and give you the strength you need. If you are in the process of letting go of someone or something in which you have felt trapped or reliant upon, don't allow insecurity or uncertainty to stop you. Deep within you know when someone or something is not worthy of your time, energy and attention. You don't need permission from anyone other than yourself to walk away from what isn't right for you, or to stand your ground and honour your values. Say no and refuse to give in to pressure. Believe that you have what it takes to stand up for your own values. Be open to help and grateful for assistance. Remember that whenever you need it, you have the power to learn, act and figure it out, and the love within will empower you to steadily move toward the life you deserve.

316

Good Magic

It's time to create your own magic. If someone is saying negative things about you, or you are thinking negative thoughts about yourself, don't believe them and don't sink to that level by lashing out. Use the positive power of your words, thoughts and intentions to override and heal meanness, fear, hate or jealousy. The Universe cannot uplift us if we are using our power or our voice to pull ourselves and others down. It is smarter, and more fun, to use your inner power to increase love and positive energy. Forgive yourself if you've lost your way. The goodness in you is more powerful than the badness in anyone or anything else. It's time to believe in goodness and magic - and you.

317

Hero

You will have days where you don't feel so heroic, but deep within you know you have guts and you know you are strong. Through challenges, the Universe shows you that you are capable of something more. Has your soul been urging you to take a step? Would you feel proud of yourself if you honoured that? Then do it. It is good to learn what it is to truly respect and take pride in yourself. In doing so you are not buying into unhelpful stories about superiority or inferiority. You are giving yourself permission to fulfil yourself as a human being, which can inspire and motivate others to learn how to do the same. Strong humans support many, whether or not they are aware of it at the time. Yet you don't need to try to impress anyone. You have everything within you to make yourself proud, to step up, and to be your own hero.

318

Normal is not for You

You are here to march to your own beat. You can choose to be at peace with yourself and passionate about your life whether others look at you with awe, admiration, confusion, fear or love - or maybe all of these at once! Being different doesn't have to mean being alone. It is only when you try to change yourself to fit in that you will lose your way and your true sense of connection. Give up allowing society to dictate the course of your life journey. The Universe doesn't want you to be someone else - it wants you to be you. Your weird streak is a proverbial breath of fresh air, preventing unimaginative collapse into the boredom of sameness. The Universe will support your every step because it enjoys you simply being you.

319

Be the Light

You are going through initiation. You are ready for it, even if it doesn't feel that way. The way to pass the test is to rely on the light within. Don't let fear or doubt make you distrust the path ahead. Don't give into despair or believe that things cannot work out. Be careful of allowing influence from those who are invested in creating pain. Have compassion for them, but do not underestimate how their negativity can taint your trust in yourself and the Universe. When we connect to the light within us, we are able to move beyond the fear and negativity in this world, and within our minds. The only thing that can trap you in negativity is the choice to believe in it. Don't choose that for yourself. The light within is more real and more powerful. Trust and be that light.

320

Elk Medicine Woman

This oracle of Elk Medicine Woman guides you to be steady on your path. Maintain the pace that matches your inner rhythms. Do not feel rushed by urgency or external demands to the point that you lose connection to your inner self and your source of innate spiritual strength. You have the endurance to go far, to attain great things in this life. Know when to conserve your energy to maintain your stamina. That might mean taking back your energy from certain worries or needless pushing to get things moving more quickly. Forcing creates resistance, which slows everything down and uses more energy. Elk Medicine Woman knows that you have the courage to go to places that most others may not dare to go. She whispers in your heart, encouraging you to believe in your potential, to work hard, but also to enjoy your life and know that when the divine timing is right, you will hit your stride. You will attain that for which you are aiming, and more.

321

An Authentic Influencer

Our world needs rebels who will redefine beauty, success and value. We need brave souls who shake up our cultural values so that we stop hurting ourselves and each other. You can decide what it really means to be beautiful, successful and worthy. That's how you take back control, disempowering toxic definitions created by mass consciousness. To live your life according to expectations of people who do not know or love you is not a recipe for happiness or inner fulfilment. Don't let the world choose your destiny for you; choose it for yourself by how you live and what you speak, daring to love and express yourself. Claiming your own values is healing medicine for our future world and the way to your bliss.

322

Black Diamond

Black diamond is the oracle of powerful spiritual mojo, indicating the power to face fears and emerge victorious. You have a transformative spiritual journey to take this lifetime. It is not always easy to take this path. However, you are a wisdom bearer. You are one of the precious ones who are not destroyed by dark experiences in life but are able to find wisdom and empowerment through overcoming them. You've done it before, and you will do it again. As your soul becomes powerful through the pressures you have survived, you'll be able to rise to even greater challenges - this time, they will feel easier for you than before. You are unstoppable. You have every right to feel bold and joyful about what life holds for you next.

323

Stirring the Cauldron

When you have an active imagination, you can forget to use it for dreaming and instead allow it to create nightmares. We can unconsciously create psychological cages to keep ourselves from taking risks that might expose us to rejection, embarrassment or failure. We can forget that when we do experience those things, they are temporary experiences only, and they can help us conquer our fears. We can actually become happier and freer through that process. We embrace more opportunities, hold ourselves back less, and more actively stir the magic and creativity of the Universe into our lives. There's a spiritual power moving through your life with intent to heal. What you are confronting is your own fear. There is no need to fear the wisdom of spiritual action in our lives. It only ever works to the greatest good.

324

Free Spirit

You have been worrying about something. There's no need to torment yourself. Everything - no matter how difficult or painful - can be worked through so that a loving and helpful outcome is ultimately realised. The free spirit within you wants to try new things, make art, express love, use your voice, without having to be perfect, without having to be certain of how it's all going to turn out. Give yourself permission to figure things out as you go. When things don't work out the way we want, we can often learn the most. It's not a punishment or a sign that you are stupid or should do something different, it's actually a sign that you are brave enough to venture into the unknown. You are such a daring spirit! Control and doubt will hold you in chains, when really, if you let yourself fly free, you'll continue to discover an amazing world and an amazing you.

325

Fierce Feminine

You are ready. Life has been preparing you. It has been your sacred coach and guide all along. Your experiences have made you stronger and wiser. You have spirit and you have courage. You are in touch with a higher energy that is loving but fierce. Trust that your inner foundations are strong, even if the ground beneath your feet seems to be shaking. When it is time to take a step, take it with confidence. When you need assistance, ask with boldness and total belief that your prayers will be answered. You have the right to say no to behaviour that is dishonest, manipulative and bullying. Rather than attack another, use your anger as inspiration to set a boundary and commit to your path. Remember that your fierceness is kindness hiding in spiritual badass clothing.

326

Lioness

There are mature souls that instinctively know how to rise above emotional game playing. They enjoy beauty as a healing energy, without allowing it to define their sense of worth. When others try to degrade them, they are strong enough to recognise that the issue rests with the other. Lioness brings you her soul medicine of honour and dignity. She stands against beauty being used as a tool of manipulation and power. She knows that taking something beautiful and distorting it into something ugly and corrupt is dishonourable behaviour. She refuses to play with the minds and emotions of others, or to be used as a pawn in another's game. She is open and direct. Even if quietly spoken, her truth has the power of a roar. The lioness claims what is rightfully hers and will not let you quit until you secure what is meant for you.

327

First This, Then That

There is a higher plan for your life path. You can accomplish it all, but not all at once. Your soul knows how to build and create, according to intelligent design. It knows that the foundations need to be laid, and the walls established before the roof can go up. Regardless of how astonishing and extraordinary the roof, if installed before the walls there would be problems! There is a certain sacred order to how things need to happen, which the soul intuitively knows. Tune in and trust your soul to show you how to manifest everything you ever dreamed of, and more, one simple step at a time. Giving value to all the steps necessary will make it a more enjoyable process. You have made more progress than you realise.

328

Sacred Dignity of the Body

The soul is the inner expression of the body and has so much to offer through the intimate sharing of your emotional and physical being. Expressions of love through the body are connected to the soul. They are a sacred gift of enormous value and worthy of appreciation and respect. It is emotional and spiritual abandonment of one's soul to deliver such gifts on demand, to take them for granted or to abuse or criticise the offerings of connection through the body. Taking, rather than receiving the gifts of love, is blasphemy against the goddess. Your body is worthy of respect. Forgive and release the past. Consider how you might truly love your body with kindness and compassion - not for how it looks or what it can do for you, but simply because it is.

329

Sanctify the Temple

Your heart is a temple for spiritual light, an inner place where grace and healing can dwell. This is very special. A temple is kept clean and pure, scented with sacred perfumes of incense, and made beautiful with our feelings of reverence and love for the spirit A temple is uncluttered and spacious to receive as much spiritual presence as possible, perhaps enough to overflow into our world, for the greater good. When spirit enters and fills the temple of the heart, things of extraordinary beauty take place. Clear your heart temple with forgiveness, gratitude and love, so that it can fulfil its destiny as a sacred channel, healing your life and the lives of those around you. This oracle predicts a great and beautiful blessing entering your life.

330

Queen of Hearts

The mind may believe that it has the power to rule, but in truth, the heart is queen. Even when the mind doesn't want to surrender to the call of the heart, fearfully listing numerous reasons why it is crazy and stupid, you know that the doubt of the mind is no match for the wisdom of the heart. As you continue to honour the heart as queen of the soul, you become a keeper of the sacred heart. That love will protect you and guide you in the most extraordinary ways. The heart has its own method and magic for attracting what it needs. Things don't have to make sense in your mind, or in anyone else's; they need to make sense to your heart. Take care of your heart and it will take care of you.

331

Oceanic

You are a rare creature, not entirely of this world. You need to swim in deeper waters, where you can commune more meaningfully with the sacred and be nourished by what is real yet cannot be explained. To deny this and remain on the logical surface of things will dry out your soul. Your soul craves mystery and magic the way many other people crave certainty and control. These yearnings are not immature or escapist. They are signs of your connection to the many worlds beyond this physical reality that intersect and influence what happens within your soul and on the planet. These are the worlds of spirit, healing, intuition, meditation and creativity. Live according to what moves you and you'll gain the independence and support that you need, whilst remaining true to yourself.

332

Shaman of Skulls

Something is ending. Perhaps it is obvious, or you may not yet be able to articulate it clearly. Either way it is a symbolic ending with a higher purpose. The shaman is spiritually trained to overcome the fear of death. Instead of avoiding endings, the shaman willingly goes through symbolic death in order to facilitate the birth of something new and important, for the greater good. Whether we want change or accept it is inevitable, the mind can still become uncertain and afraid. We may become confused and cling to what is ending. These are natural human responses to loss. Be patient, be kind, but also be strong. What is happening for you now is in alignment with a higher purpose and loving plan. You have the spiritual strength to move through it. Be encouraged. You have the capacity to rise from the depths of darkness, stepping forward on your life path with more wisdom, empowerment and determination than ever before. Give yourself the chance to continue and you will succeed.

333

On Your Own Terms

You are not the person you once were. You know it, but others might not always be ready to let the old you go so easily. Do not allow yourself to be pushed back into old patterns of behaviour that are not true to who you are now. You have worked hard to grow and become this new self. Believe that this is more real than the past. Others may offer input, but when it all comes down to it, it is you alone making your life decisions. Sometimes this means standing your ground and reinforcing, to yourself and others, that this is how you are living your life from now on. You get to choose how you want to feel, how you want to live, and who you want to be. You're ready for the responsibility and the reward of living your life on your own terms.

ABOUT THE AUTHOR

Alana Fairchild

From the earliest memories I have, I was always in conscious connection with Spirit. It has always been as natural as breathing to me. When something is natural for you, especially if it has been that way since childhood, you can assume for a long time it is natural for everyone. It took me some years to realise my sensitivity, healing ability and natural conscious connection to the spiritual was unusual and could help people. So, I chose to create beautiful offerings to support humans in discovering and manifesting the truth of their hearts.

333

Books, oracle decks, music albums, guided meditations, training programs for healers and more. All are designed to bring out the beauty and truth of your inner divine nature, so you can live with freedom, courage, happiness and peace. If you would like to find out more, please visit me at my online home, www.alanafairchild.com.